Health and Social Care

for Intermediate GNVQ

WITHDRAWN

2nd edition

Health and Social Care

for Intermediate GNVQ

Liam Clarke

stanley thornes GNVQ

First published in 1995 by:
Stanley Thornes (Publishers) Ltd
Delta Place
27 Bath Road
CHELTENHAM
GL53 7TH
United Kingdom

Second edition published 2000

00 01 02 03 04 / 10 9 8 7 6 5 4 3 2

A catalogue record for this book is available from the British Library

ISBN 0 7487 3508 9

Line illustrations by Angela Lumley

Typeset by Florence Production Ltd, Stoodleigh, Devon
Printed and bound in Spain by Graficas Estella S.A.

Contents

Acknowledgements

The author and publisher would like to acknowledge the advice of Peter Scourfield and Carol Hicks, who provided extremely useful comments on the manuscript throughout the writing process.

The author and publishers are grateful to the following for permission to reproduce previously published material:

- Alzheimer's Disease Society – p. 14 (right).
- Foodlink – p. 150 (bottom left). Produced by Food and Drink Federation, 6 Catherine Street, London WC2B 5JJ.
- Health Education Authority – pp. 82, 107, 118, 122, 140 and 150 (top left and top right). © Health Education Authority.
- Her Majesty's Stationery Office - pp. 116 and 150 (bottom right). Crown copyright material is reproduced with the permission of the Controller of Her Majesty's Stationery Office.
- National Meningitis Trust – p. 14 (left). Reproduced by kind permission of the National Meningitis Trust.

Every attempt has been made to contact copyright holders, and we apologise if any have been overlooked. Should copyright have been unwittingly infringed in this book, the owners should contact the publishers who will make corrections at reprint.

Photo credits

- John Birdsall (www.JohnBirdsall.co.uk) – pp. 35 and 99.
- Angela Hampton - Family Life Picture Library – pp. 25, 34, 67 and 91.

Assessment for GNVQ

GNVQs are alternative qualifications to A levels or GCSEs and can be taken at three
levels:

Foundation
- **Part One GNVQ (Foundation)** – equivalent to two GCSEs at grades D–G
- **Foundation GNVQ** – equivalent to four GCSEs at grades D–G; these
  normally take one year of full-time study

Intermediate
- **Part One GNVQ (Intermediate)** – equivalent to two GCSEs at grades A–C
- **Intermediate GNVQ** – equivalent to four GCSEs at grades A–C; these
  normally take one year of full-time study

Advanced
- **Advanced GNVQ (called 'vocational A levels')**
  - **Full award (12 units)** – equivalent to two A levels; these are normally
    taken over a two-year period of full-time study
  - **Single award (6 units)** – equivalent to one A level; these are normally
    taken over a one-year period of full-time study
  - **Three-unit awards** – these have been designed to encourage students to
    study GNVQs alongside other qualifications such as A levels, AS levels or
    GCSEs

How is a GNVQ structured?

All GNVQ courses are made up of units:

- **Mandatory** – these are units you must study
- **Optional units** – these are units you choose to study

What is in a GNVQ unit?

All Intermediate GNVQ units are of equal size and value and are organised in the same way.

You will be provided with a set of specifications from your awarding body. **Section 1** tells you about the unit and gives you brief headings of what you will learn about. For example:

Unit 1: Health, social care and early years provision

About this unit

You will learn

- about the main roles of people who work in the health, social care and early years services and the structures within which they function
- the care value base that underpins all health and social care work with clients
- about the skills that are needed by people working in health, social care and early years services
- the basic communication skills that are needed by people working in the health, social care and early years services

It will also tell you how the unit will be assessed, for example:

Units 1 and 2 are assessed through your portfolio work and the grade that you get for that work is the grade for the unit. Unit 3 will be assessed through external assessment (a test or examination set by the awarding body) and marked by that body. The grade for the external test will be the grade for the unit.

Section 2 tells you in more detail what you will need to learn. For example:

The care value base

You will need to learn about the care 'value base' because it underpins the work of all people who work in health, social care and early years services. You will appreciate and understand how the care value base helps empower clients by:

- promoting antidiscriminatory practice
- maintaining the confidentiality of information
- promoting and supporting individuals' rights to dignity, independence, health and safety
- acknowledging individuals' personal beliefs and identity

- supporting individuals through alternative approaches, for example identifying alternative approaches if the first is not effective
- minimising obstacles to communication, using communication aids, translators and advocates

Section 3 is called Assessment Evidence. This section will tell you what you have to do to gain a pass, merit or distinction. For example:

You need to produce a service profile based on two different health and/or social care settings, which includes

- the organisation of the services and the roles of people who work in them
- how the care value base underpins work in supporting clients
- relevant codes of practice or charters
- ways in which different types of communication skills are used in care settings

To achieve a pass you must show you understand and can use relevant information to:

- correctly identify the care sector and client group for each setting
- thoroughly explore the roles of two workers, correctly identify and explain the care value base that underpins their work
- describe the use of any codes of practice or charters that relate to the organisation in which the workers are based
- show your ability to use relevant communication skills and give accurate explanation of possible barriers to communication with clients.

To achieve a merit you must also show you can:

- analyse the job roles that you have chosen and compare the way in which the care value base is implemented in day-to-day work in the two different settings
- explain fully how the codes of practice and charters help to protect users of the services
- give an explanation of the communication methods you chose to use, identifying your strengths and weaknesses.

To achieve a distinction you must also show you can:

- show a high level of understanding of the care settings and the work roles of staff in these settings by explaining how work roles are influenced by the sector and type of organisation
- show realistic proposals for improving your communication skills
- give an evaluation of the effectiveness of codes of practice and charters in upholding the care value base.

What is the Intermediate GNVQ in Health and Social Care?

The Intermediate GNVQ is made up of:

- Three **mandatory vocational units** (these are units you must do)
  - **Unit 1: Health, social care and early years provision**
  - **Unit 2: Promoting health and well-being**
  - **Unit 3: Understanding personal development**. This unit is externally tested. This means that an external body, such as BTEC, City & Guilds or RSA, sets a test paper that you must pass to gain the unit. The grade that you get for the test will be the grade that you will get for the unit. No other assessment will take place for this unit.
- **Optional units**, which are devised by the individual awarding bodies. These optional units differ from one awarding body to another.

Intermediate Units can be studied separately and can be passed one at a time. If you leave a course or transfer to a school or college in another part of the country you will be credited with the units that you have already passed. This means that you will only have to complete the units that you have not already passed to gain the GNVQ. You do not have do the whole qualification over again.

How are GNVQs assessed?

Assessment for GNVQs focuses on what you have actually achieved. This is called outcome-based assessment. Your assessors (teachers) will assess your work after you have given them evidence that you have achieved what they have asked you to do. For example, in Unit 1 you will be asked to :

- identify the two health/care sectors that you have chosen and identify the client group(s) they support. Describe the purpose of each service, showing how it fits into the national framework.
- clearly describe the roles of two workers (one from each setting you have chosen), correctly explaining how the care value base underpins their work
- identify and describe the use of any codes of practice or charters that relate to the organisations in which your chosen workers are based
- identify the different forms of communication skills used in the care settings, describing their purposes.

When you have done this and provided enough evidence, usually in writing, then your assessors will judge your work against national standards to see if you have met them. If you have provided enough evidence at the right standard then you will gain a pass. When you have:

- analysed the job roles that you have chosen and compared the way in which the care value base is implemented in day-to-day work in the two different settings
- explained how codes of practice and charters help to protect users of the services
- explained how the different communication skills used in the care settings provide support for clients, identifying any possible barriers

you will gain a merit, and when you have:

- analysed the effectiveness of the codes of practice and charters in upholding the care value base from both the clients' and care workers' perspective
- evaluated the communication strategies used in the care settings, identifying strengths and ways of improving any weakness

you will gain a distinction.

Your written work is checked by your teacher (assessor) and if it is not up to standard the assessor will discuss with you how you can obtain the missing evidence. Remember, you can try as many times as you like to reach the required standard. No time limits can be put on you to complete the work. GNVQs are designed so that each student can work at their own pace. Some may gather evidence in a short period; others may take longer.

Your assessor will judge the evidence you have presented for each unit and ensure that your completed work meets the required national standard.

Internal assessment

This is the assessment that takes place within your school or college. We will look a little later at what a portfolio of evidence is and what should go into it. Your teacher will support you in preparing your portfolio. Assessors have to be qualified and have adequate knowledge of the area they are working in. Their work is checked (verified) by another experienced teacher (assessor) called an internal verifier. The internal verifier selects some of your work and checks that it has met the national standards. Verification will also ensure that all the assessment within a school or college is consistent with the national standards. The work of the internal verifier is also checked by an external verifier, who is appointed by BTEC, City & Guilds or RSA to ensure that assessors and internal verifiers are working consistently to national standards. The external verifier will visit your school or college at least twice a year and will usually see some of your work and talk to you about it.

External assessment

This will consist of written tests set by external bodies, such as BTEC, for roughly one-third of your total GNVQ. The written tests will assess the skills and knowledge that you have gained during the time you have been studying the unit content. Each GNVQ written test paper lasts about one hour; the pass mark is usually 70%.

All the awarding bodies (BTEC, City & Guilds, RSA) must ensure that assessment can be undertaken by all students, including those with learning difficulties.

Preparing for assessment

Your portfolio of evidence and the external tests for the appropriate units will need to be completed and passed in order for the unit to be credited towards the full GNVQ award. Evidence may be obtained in a variety of ways, including:

- **Practical tests**. Be familiar with what you are going to be tested on and have ready all equipment and materials you will need. Do not rush, and remember to work to health and safety guidelines. Always make sure that what you are doing is safe, both for you and for any other person. Your assessor will have given you clear guidelines as to what you have to do to reach the required standard.
- **Assignments and projects**. Plan your time carefully; take time drawing up your action plan; discuss your work with your teacher or lecturer. Try to achieve all the things you set yourself to do in your action plan. Make sure your work is neat and well presented. Each assignment or project will include clear written guidelines of what you have to do to achieve a pass. These guidelines will also have been discussed with you and you will have had an opportunity to question them.
- **Observation**. You may be observed either by one of your own classmates or by a teacher. They will observe you to see how you carry out certain tasks – how you behave in groups, if you can organise other people, for instance. Try not to feel uncomfortable when being observed.
- **Oral questioning**. This is a common way to find out if you can tell your assessor why you have done certain things. What you have written or done in groups may not be clear – your assessor will ask you questions to allow you to explain and talk more about your evidence.
- **Written external tests**. Understand the process of revision – ask your teacher to explain the best way for you to revise. Start revising for written tests early. Revising is easier if you have made clear and complete notes. Always read the instructions on the test papers carefully and remember to take your time.

Is it possible to appeal against the assessment decision of my assessor?

Each school or college **must** have an appeals procedure that will deal effectively with any complaints a student may have. This appeals procedure is different from the complaints procedure described in your college student handbook. There must be an appeals procedure for GNVQ courses. You can appeal on the grounds that an assessment procedure was not properly carried out or that an outcome (pass) was not carried out in a proper manner. Ask your teacher or lecturer for a copy of the appeals procedure – you are entitled to a copy at the beginning of the course.

Organising a portfolio of evidence

What is a portfolio?

Your portfolio will usually be kept in a large A4 ring binder. All your written evidence, assignments, projects, photographs, drawings, etc. will be kept in the binder. You must also keep a list (index) in the binder of other evidence, such as video tapes, sound recordings, large drawings, etc., that is kept somewhere else. This is so that the assessor, internal verifier and external verifier know that this evidence exists and can find it.

A portfolio is a convenient way to keep a record and to present evidence that you have collected. It is a permanent record of the evidence of your achievements over the year. The evidence that you have collected will allow you to demonstrate to your assessors that you have achieved the skills, knowledge and understanding to gain the Intermediate GNVQ qualification.

Your portfolio should be organised into sections, each section containing evidence for one unit. The portfolio will also contain forms completed by your assessor. These forms will contain basic information about the status of your evidence for each unit.

The index to your portfolio should include:

- Name and details of class
- List of sections
  Unit 1: Health, social care and early years provision
  Unit 2: Promoting health and well-being
  Unit 3: Understanding personal development
  Unit 4: Optional units
  List of supplementary evidence
  Units that the supplementary evidence relates to

Providing evidence for your portfolio

There are two types of evidence:

- **Performance evidence**. Sometimes called direct evidence, this may consist of a report, assignment, a product (a toy, for example) or an assessor's written report of observation of something you have done.
- **Supplementary or indirect evidence**. This may consist of photographs, video tapes, audio tapes, evidence of written or oral questioning, tests or references from workplace supervisors.

Remember that work, class notes, etc. that do not provide evidence should not be kept in your portfolio.

Evidence should arise as a result of the work you have been asked to do by your assessor and you agreed to do after drawing up your action plan. How much and what evidence you require will be discussed with you. It would be helpful to have an action plan to help you organise how you are going to collect evidence.

Example of action plan

You have been asked to find out what health and social care services are available in your locality for children with learning difficulties and when you have done this to present a verbal report to your group.

Action plan

Task	*How*	*By when*
Find out about services	Talk to lecturer	Now
	Look up Yellow Pages and telephone directory	1st February
	Ring local SSD and hospital	2nd February
	Visit local health centre	5th February
Write report	Draft report to lecturer	10th February
	Final report	20th February
Prepare talk	Get OHPs from lecturer	22nd February
	Prepare OHPs	26th February
	Write talk	26th February
Give talk	See that room is set out	1st March
	Is OHP working?, etc.	
Review action plan	Did I meet my plans?	

Remember...

- Present your portfolio in a professional manner.
- All the evidence that you are providing should be sufficient (enough), authentic (your own work) and relevant (test what the performance criteria ask to be tested).
- The assessor and verifiers should find the portfolio easy to read, understand and access. The index should identify what the evidence refers to.
- The documentation should be easy to read.
- Before you present your portfolio, remember that you will be asked questions about it by the assessor and the internal and external verifier.
- You should know exactly what is in your portfolio, as you could be asked to explain the evidence to the external verifier.

Key Skills units

- **Communication**
- **Application of number**
- **Information technology**

Key Skills units can be studied separately, but the skills in these units can be taught and tested in assignments or projects set for the Intermediate Units. It is important to remember that you do not need to obtain Key Skills to pass the Intermediate GNVQ in Health and Social Care. It is now a separate qualification from Key Skills.

Health, social care and early years provision

What is covered in this unit

1.1 **The main roles of people who work in the health, social care and early years services and the structures within which they function**

1.2 **The care value base**

1.3 **Skills needed by people working in health, social care and early years services**

1.4 **Basic communication skills needed by people working in health, social care and early years services**

At the end of this unit you will be asked to produce a report based on two health and/or social care services. If you would like to see further details of the tasks you are likely to need to carry out for assessment please refer to the end of the unit where an assignment has been set (see pp. 71–2). This unit will guide you through what you need to know in order to successfully put together this report. You will be assessed on this work and awarded a grade. This grade will contribute to the overall grade you will get for Unit One.

Materials you will need to complete this unit

- Local authority Community Care Plan
- NHS leaflets
- Local information from voluntary and private care organisations
- Local and national charters and codes of practice
- Information from your local careers library
- Access to the Internet
  - Open Government site (www.open.gov.uk) gives information on latest government developments (Acts, Green Papers, etc.)
  - Local authority and local health authority sites, which give information, statistics etc.

1.1 The main roles of people who work in the health, social care and early years services and the structures within which they function

Health care services

We may all work hard at maintaining our health and independence, but there are times when medical or social care is necessary. The UK at the beginning of the 21st century has a system of free health care – the National Health Service (NHS). Health care has not always been free, however, and indeed some people today choose to pay into private health care schemes.

Health services before 1948

To fully understand the NHS today it is important to appreciate its origins. Before 1948, most doctors worked privately and people had to pay for treatment. Many people took out insurance, through friendly societies and trade unions, for example, to help financially in times of illness.

If anyone needed hospital treatment they had to go into one of four types of institution:

- psychiatric hospitals (or 'asylums' as they were then called), for people with mental health problems
- isolation hospitals (also known as sanatoriums or fever hospitals), for people with infectious diseases such as tuberculosis (TB)
- voluntary hospitals (such as Manchester Royal Infirmary, Guy's Hospital)
- workhouse hospitals for those who could not afford to pay for health care. Conditions in workhouse hospitals were very poor and many people feared them.

Activity 1

a Use the local history section of your main library and try to find out about the beginnings of hospitals and health services in your locality.

b Arrange to talk to an elderly person about health care before the NHS.

Discuss with your class colleagues the accounts you have been given.

The National Health Service 1948–1990

In 1948, Aneurin Bevan, the Minister for Health in the Labour government, set up a free health service across the country in an attempt to provide fair access to health and care for everyone. This new National Health Service brought all the various health and care services under the control of the Ministry of Health. Funding for the service was to come from general taxation, National Insurance contributions and charges made to private patients.

The National Health and Community Care Act 1990

This Act was the result of a number of proposals put forward in 1989 in a government White Paper *Working for Change*.

Purchasers and providers (the internal market)

The White Paper proposed that there should be competition between hospitals and other service **providers** such as Social Services departments and general practitioners (GPs). The government thought that competition between services would improve things. It proposed that District Health Authorities (DHAs) should be **purchasers**, having the responsibility for buying services for patients, using funds given to them by the government based on the population in their area (taking into account factors such as age, sex, etc.). Hospitals contracted with GPs to provide services. The aim was to make the providers of the services (hospitals) more responsive and more efficient as they would have to compete with one another for patients. As a result, 'money followed patients', as GPs paid for services used by their patients. DHAs also purchased services (such as specialist services or beds in nursing homes) from public, private and voluntary providers.

Health care trusts

Hospitals, and other units such as ambulance services, opted out of health authority control and became self-governing trusts with responsibility for their own budgets.

Family Health Service Authorities

Family Practitioner Committees became Family Health Service Authorities (FHSAs), accountable to the Regional Health Authorities rather than directly to the Ministry of Health. FHSAs disappeared in 1996.

Fundholding GP practices

GP practices with large numbers of patients received money directly from the Regional Health Authority to purchase a defined range of services for their patients. These included outpatient services, diagnostic tests and inpatient and day-care treatments, for which it was possible for the GP or patient to choose the time and place. This system allowed GPs to buy services from local and regional hospitals that best suited the individual needs of their patients and gave the best value for money. GPs could choose which hospital (provider) a patient went to, or which

quick fire

What do the initials DHA stand for?

3

consultant (provider) treated them, because the GP was paying for (purchasing) the service. The Health Act 1999 abolished the **GP fundholder**.

Community care

Government proposals in 1981 had called for local authorities to be given the lead in planning community care, thus linking personal Social Services more strongly with health issues.

As with most legislation relating to health and care, the National Health Service and Community Care Act came into force gradually. One of the earliest effects was the formation of 56 hospital trusts in April 1991, with a further 95 hospital and service trusts in 1992. In April 1991, 306 fundholding GP practices were also established. The structure of the NHS in 1991 is shown in the diagram below.

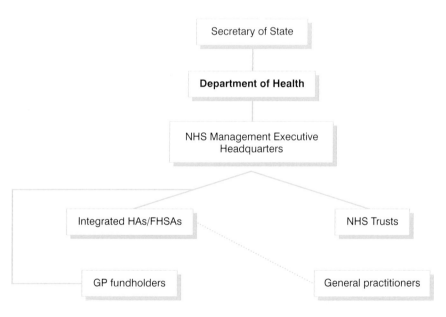

The structure of the National Health Service 1991

How is the health service paid for?

The cost of the health service for the whole of the UK in 1997 was £34.7 billion, more than £1600 for every household in the country. Almost 96% of this money comes from direct taxation (income tax and National Insurance). Only a very small proportion of the cost comes from charges. Nearly 80% of prescriptions are dispensed free of charge. The NHS spends over £4 billion a year on medicines. Over 40% of what is spent each year goes on the over-65s, although they only represent about 17% of the population.

quick fire

Where does the money to pay for the health service come from?

Health, social care and early years services 2000

The Health Act 1999

The Act's main purpose was to make changes to the way in which the National Health Service is run. It abolished GP fundholding in England, Wales and Northern Ireland. It amended the National Health Service Act 1977 to make provision for the setting up of new statutory bodies in England and Wales, to be known as **Primary Care Groups** (PCGs).

In 1997, the new Labour government set out to change the structure of the NHS in order to provide an up-to-date, quicker and more responsive service. The government stated its commitment in a White Paper, *The New NHS – Modern, Dependable*, to provide a service based on people's need and not on ability to pay. This new service is based on:

- making it easier and faster for people to get advice and information about health, illness and the NHS so that they can better care for themselves and their families. 'NHS Direct', a 24-hour telephone advice line staffed by nurses (who advise patients), is available across the whole country.
- swift advice and treatment in the community in local surgeries and health centres, with GPs working alongside other health care staff to provide a wide range of services
- prompt access to specialist services in hospital linked to local surgeries and health centres.

What do the initials PCG stand for?

The government believed that the service that operated under the National Health and Community Care Act 1990 meant that decisions were made by too many different people and caused unfairness to some patients (many GPs did not become fundholders, for example). To replace this system the government wanted to move away from outright competition to a more collaborative approach, delivering a national service against national standards and working more closely with local authorities so that patients' needs would be at the centre of the process. All these ideas were incorporated into the Health Act 1999.

Health authorities

Under the Health Act 1999, over a period of time health authorities will relinquish their direct commissioning (buying services) roles to Primary Care Groups. Health authorities, working with local authorities, **NHS Trusts** and Primary Care Groups, will take the lead in drawing up three-year Health Improvement Programmes, which will provide the framework within which all NHS bodies will operate.

GP fundholding

GP fundholding ceased to exist in England, Wales and Northern Ireland in March 1999.

5

England

Primary Care Groups

PCGs became a reality on 1 April 1999, when 481 groups were set up in England. A number of these groups only advise the health authority on commissioning care for its population. Others (called Level 2 Groups) take responsibility for managing the healthcare budget in their area, acting as part of the health authority. The board of the Primary Health Care Group can transfer money between hospital and community services in order to use the money where it believes it is needed most.

Primary Care Groups are run by boards, the members including GPs and other professionals such as nurses and hospital doctors. They employ staff to develop and implement policy. The population they serve can vary from 206 000 people in York to 54 467 people in Wakefield (south).

Primary Care Group board

The PCG board is accountable to the health authority and will consist of:

- GPs (between four and seven) – the Chairperson is usually a GP
- nurses (community and practice nurses) – up to two
- a member of the health authority
- a lay member of the community
- a representative from the Social Services department.

What will PCGs do?

- Improve the health of the community and address health inequalities in it.
- Develop primary care and community health services in their areas.
- Improve the quality of care provided by helping GPs and their health providers to deliver and integrate services.
- Advise about or undertake commissioning of hospital services for patients so as to meet appropriately patients' needs.

It is proposed that some of these PCGs will eventually become trusts.

Primary Health Groups

Primary Health Groups, made up of GPs and community nurses, will work with NHS Trusts to plan the new services to deliver prompt, accessible (easy-to-get-at), seamless (without breaks) care of a high standard. These groups will work to set quality standards agreed between health authorities and Primary Care Groups.

What is a PCG?

What is a Primary Health Group?

NHS Trusts

NHS Trusts will provide patient care in hospital and in the community under long-term agreements with Primary Care Groups.

The new National Health Service 1999

Health authorities

Health authorities have a number of key tasks:

- to assess the health needs of the local population
- to develop a plan for meeting those needs
- to decide on the range of services necessary to meet needs
- to allocate resources to Primary Care Groups
- to make Primary Care Groups do their job.

Health Action Zones

To give priority to areas of greatest need, the government has set up Health Action Zones to help reduce these inequalities. Health Action Zones will bring together local health organisations with local authorities, community groups, voluntary groups and local business to produce an improvement in the health of local people that can be measured and sustained.

What organisations will make up a Health Action Zone?

Hospital and specialist services

Some 280 major hospitals in England provide a service to a range of people. Hospitals are traditionally seen as institutions where people who are too ill to be cared for at home go for treatment as an inpatient or an outpatient. In hospitals, the medical personnel are organised into teams of doctors whose role is to diagnose, prescribe and monitor the success or otherwise of treatment. A person is normally referred to a hospital specialist by his or her GP. Many are initially seen by the specialist in a clinic as outpatients following this **referral**, or they may go into hospital for inpatient treatment.

The hospital medical teams are supported by personnel from other disciplines, such as radiographers, occupational therapists and physiotherapists, whose specialist knowledge and skills allow them to provide services to help the doctor in diagnosis and treatment. Teams including such personnel are known as multidisciplinary teams.

What does the term multidisciplinary team mean?

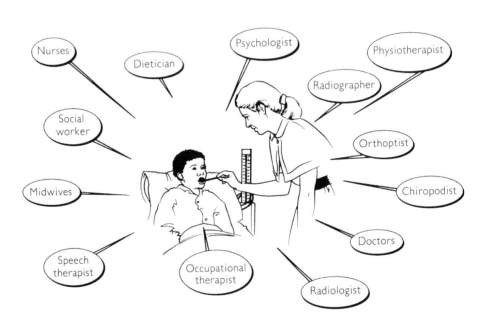

The multidisciplinary team

Local Health Group Boards – Wales

Local Health Group Boards are the equivalent in Wales of the Primary Care Groups in England. Unlike in England, GPs are not in a majority on these groups. The groups have the same boundaries as the 22 Local Health Authorities. They are health authority subcommittees and to begin with will simply have an advisory role. The new Welsh Assembly will make the final decision as to the future role of these groups.

Health Reforms in Northern Ireland

New reforms set out in the paper *Fit for the Future: A New Approach* are proposed for Northern Ireland. Health reforms in Northern Ireland will be delayed until the Northern Ireland Assembly takes shape. GP fundholding will be abolished in 2000 if and when the new structures are to be introduced.

Health and social care partnerships will be set up consisting of Primary Care Co-operatives (PCCs) serving 50 000–100 000 people. These groups will assess health and social care needs in their area and oversee health and well-being improvement programmes.

PCCs will hold budgets for commissioning health and social services, for drugs and for staff and premises. It is expected that at least three years' development will be necessary before they become fully functioning.

Social care services

Social Services departments (SSDs) are run by local authorities to provide community-based services available to all, with a strong orientation towards the family. The main objective of a Social Services department is to support people in their own homes and enable them to care for themselves and their families and dependants. SSDs will be expected to plan services very closely with Programme Planning Groups.

The department also purchases accommodation, particularly for the elderly, people with disabilities and children who cannot remain in their own home.

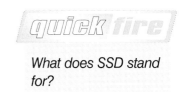

What does SSD stand for?

The Social Services team

The Social Services Committee, established by the Local Authority and Social Services Act 1970, has responsibility for four areas:

- child care, under the various children's acts and adoption acts, including the Children Act 1989
- provision and regulation of residential accommodation for older people and people with disabilities, under the National Assistance Act 1948 and the Registered Homes Act 1984
- welfare services for older people, people with disabilities and those who are chronically ill
- statutory powers under the various Mental Health Acts.

The Committee also has power to delegate some responsibilities to other organisations (usually voluntary organisations) and to provide necessary assistance.

A typical structure of a local authority Social Services department in England is shown in the diagram below.

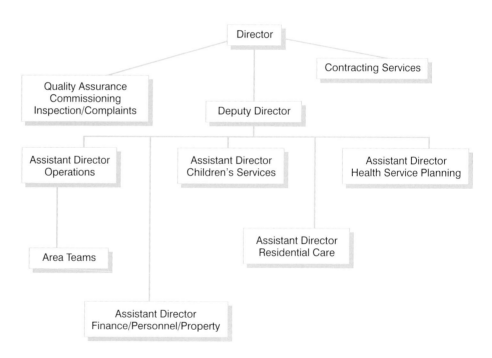

Typical structure of a local authority Social Services department

Key Skills

You can use Activity 2 to provide evidence for Key Skills Communication C2.2

Activity 2

a Obtain a copy of your local Community Care Plan or Health Improvement Programme. You can get this from your local SSD or library.

b Find out what services or provision the Plan or Programme has provided for minority groups in the locality.

How do people gain access to health and social care services?

There are basically three ways that a person can be referred to the health or social care services. These are:

- self-referral
- referral through professionals
- compulsory referral.

Self-referral

This is the first route for most people receiving health and social care. In the health service it may simply involve turning up at the GP's or dentist's surgery. The first point of contact might also be through a health visitor, for example.

In social care, self-referral may involve contacting the duty social worker in a local Social Services office or going directly to a care facility, such as a day-care centre or a nursery.

In all cases the initiative is with the person requiring care, or a friend or relative, who makes the initial contact. An example of the latter case might be the partner of a person who is depressed seeking professional help for them.

Referral through a professional

Unless they are admitted to hospital as an accident or emergency case, the only way that a person may voluntarily receive hospital treatment is by being referred by another professional, normally a GP. Where a GP diagnoses, or suspects, ill-health that requires specialist treatment, they refer the patient to an outpatient clinic. In more urgent cases, the GP may arrange direct admission to a ward.

In social care, an example of referral by a professional might be when a teacher in a school suspects child abuse and refers the case to the Social Services duty social worker. Under the Children Act 1989 all schools must have a named person who is responsible for doing this. Other examples might be a police officer who has given a 'warning' to a child who has committed an offence and feels that the child should be referred to Social Services, or a health visitor who suspects that a child may be being abused and should be referred to the SSD.

quick fire

Name two professionals who could refer people for services.

Compulsory referral

Some people may have no choice about whether or not they are referred for support or treatment. Severely mentally ill people can be referred compulsorily, under the Mental Health Act, as can children who are at risk, under the various pieces of child care legislation.

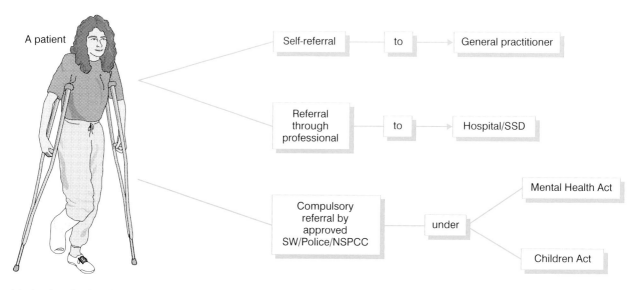

Methods of referral or access to services

How can the health and social care and early years services meet people's needs?

How are the needs of client groups met by the health and social care services? We will look at each client group in turn:

- families
- people with disabilities
- children
- elderly people.

How do the health, social care and early years services meet the needs of families?

Most people understand that 'family' refers to a group of people who are related to one another by blood and/or marriage (or other similar relationship). Everyone knows what a family is – mum, dad, brothers, sisters, grandparents. There is no doubt that families are now smaller than they used to be. The average number of children per family dropped from 2.3 in 1970 to 1.8 in the 1990s.

quick fire

What does the term 'family' mean?

People living alone are not considered to be a family. Between 1961 and 1992 the number of people living alone increased by nearly 300%.

There was a fourfold increase in one-parent families from 2.5% in 1971 to over 10% by the early 1990s.

One-parent families 1971–91, by sex of parent

| | No. of families | | |
	1971	1979	1991
Female	520 000	760 000	1 200 000
Male	100 000	100 000	100 000
Total one-parent families	620 000	860 000	1 300 000

Note: The 1.3 million one-parent families in 1991 contained approximately 2.2 million dependent chidren

There is a difference in the spread of one-parent families in the UK. One in 10 families in the North of England, West Midlands, North-west and Wales consists of a lone parent with dependent children, compared to 1 in 14 in East Anglia and Northern Ireland.

All of these figures point to a decline in the number of 'traditional' families (married couples with dependent children).

Activity 3

a List the factors you think might contribute to the difference in the numbers of one-parent families in different regions of the UK.
b How could this change affect the ability of the NHS to meet the needs of families?

Discuss your ideas with your class colleagues.

Key Skills

You can use Activity 3 to provide evidence for Key Skills Communication C2.1a and C2.3

These changes are making it more difficult for the family to provide the full range of personal care required by dependent groups. The steady increase in the number of one-parent families may be due to the fact that a woman with dependent children no longer feels that she needs to stay with her husband. However, as a single parent she is still likely to suffer insecurity and loss of income. The increase in one-parent families, and the disruption it brings to married life, not only increases the demand on the social care services but also makes it more difficult for families to provide informal care for older people and those with disabilities.

Informal carers – the family and the care of dependent members

An estimated 5.7 million adults are caring for less capable friends and relatives at home (informal carers). Around one-quarter of them spend more than 20 hours per week caring for a dependent relative, and of this quarter approximately 60% spend 60 hours a week. One adult in eight is providing informal care in one in six households.

Women are more likely to be carers than men but the difference is not very marked – 14% compared with 11%. Informal carers are ordinary, untrained people doing an exacting job and they have ordinary people's needs and feelings. They may need support from the Social Services and health services because of feelings of loneliness and isolation and because of inability to do heavy jobs, such as lifting or bathing.

Informal carers often have a sense of individual, rather than shared and collective, responsibility for their dependent relatives. Many of them suffer physical and emotional stress and ill-health themselves because of lack of support from the statutory services. When they become ill, the person they are caring for is often left without support. One of the key objectives of the National Health Service and Community Care Act 1990 was the support of informal carers, although it still remains to be seen if this occurs to any great extent.

The Carers Recognition and Services Act 1995 (which amended the Community Care Act 1990) placed a duty on local authority Social Services departments to assess the ability of a carer to provide, and to continue providing care. SSDs have a duty to take this into account when deciding what services a person might need.

Carers need support too

Activity 4

Visit your local Social Services department or obtain your local Community Care Plan and:

a Find out what types of support your local SSD offers to informal carers.
b List the different kinds of self-help group available in your local community to help carers in their own homes.

How do the health, social care and early years services meet the needs of people with disabilities?

Over 200 000 people in England are blind or partially sighted. Some 1.3 million people are registered as substantially or permanently disabled, most of them people who are over 65. Many people are cared for in residential homes. Almost 250 000 elderly and younger people are cared for in local authority, private or voluntary homes.

The main legislation that enables local authorities to support people with disabilities in the community is the Chronically Sick and Disabled Persons Act 1970. For the purposes of the Act, chronically sick or disabled persons are those who are 'substantially and permanently handicapped' by illness, injury, congenital deformity or old age. The Act enables the local authority to provide:

- practical assistance in the home – in obtaining radio, telephone, TV or library services
- works or adaptations in the home
- assistance with holidays
- meals at home.

What is disability?

There are so many types of disability that the term cannot be defined easily. Disabilities may be the result of:

- genetic or inherited disorders, such as muscular dystrophy and Down's syndrome
- damage at birth, such as cerebral palsy
- accidents (causing brain damage or paralysis, for example)
- illnesses (such as bronchitis) or disorders (such as Alzheimer's disease) that have occurred during a person's lifetime.

Disability may be either:

- physical, such as arthritis, chronic heart disease, muscular dystrophy, multiple sclerosis, blindness or deafness, or
- mental (now more usually termed learning difficulty), such as Down's syndrome or cerebral palsy in children, or dementia in elderly people.

15

Chronic disability is a condition that develops slowly over a long period, or which lasts a long time, or a condition that is incurable. *Acute disability* is a condition that occurs suddenly, which may be severe and may last for a relatively short time. A *congenital disability* is a non-hereditary condition present at birth.

There are degrees of disability. Some people with disabilities, for example, may be able to cope and live at home, while others with the same disability may need much support and may even need residential care. When discussing support services for people with disabilities we need to keep in mind that each person reacts differently to the same disability. For this reason we must always regard each client as an individual and focus on their individual needs, both physical and emotional, rather than on their disability.

Value judgements

In the past and, to some extent, even today, services for people with disabilities have been developed on the basis of prejudice and hearsay. They focus on a person's inabilities, rather than on what they *can* do. People with disabilities are often seen as objects of derision, dread or pity, and as a burden to society. People with learning disabilities are often denied reasonable access to services. For example, people object to the building of hostels for such people in their neighbourhood.

How do health, social care and early years services meet the needs of children?

The proportion of the population under 15 years of age decreased between 1971 and the mid-1980s – in 1981 it was one in five. In contrast, however, as we shall see later, the population over 65 years of age has risen considerably. This means that the total dependent population (children and elderly people) is approximately 30% of the total population. As the elderly population increases, there will be more and more pressure on social care and health services and less demand for schools.

Learning difficulties

Until recently, children with learning difficulties used to be termed 'mentally handicapped'. Many factors can cause learning disability. For example, a chromosomal defect causes Down's syndrome, while other factors, such as infections or injury, may cause brain damage.

Cerebral palsy

Severely brain-damaged children may also suffer from cerebral palsy, or spastic paralysis. This is a non-progressive disorder of the brain that impairs daily living activities. The regions of the brain that control movement and muscle tension are affected, producing spasticity

16

(or stiffness), floppiness, weakness, involuntary movements or unsteadiness. Children who suffer from cerebral palsy find it difficult to demonstrate their intellectual powers and many such children in the past were misdiagnosed as learning disabled.

It is important for families to be encouraged to help such children to develop their intellectual skills by providing them with a stimulating environment and opportunities to learn, though their ability to move is limited. Children with cerebral palsy may have problems with communicating. Electronic communication systems using voice synthesisers and computers have opened up a whole range of opportunities to communicate for people with speech difficulties.

Deafness

Deafness is more common among children who have learning disability than in those who do not. Deafness may make children appear to be more learning disabled than they are, so a full assessment of the child's needs and capabilities is important. The most frequent cause of deafness is nerve deafness resulting from the brain damage that also caused the learning disability. In many cases, the child will have missed out on a great deal of speech experience as a result of inadequate hearing.

Blindness

This is another disorder that is common among children with learning disability.

Epilepsy

Epilepsy is probably the most common associated disorder that occurs in children with learning disability. Epilepsy is not linked in any way to intellectual disability but it can cause a major setback in the child's progress. A major fit is a very frightening thing for a parent to see. In fact, children rarely come to harm during a fit and attacks look much worse than they really are.

Hydrocephalus and spina bifida

Hydrocephalus (fluid on the brain) and spina bifida (split spine) are not on their own causes of mental disability.

Spina bifida is a congenital abnormality caused by the two halves of the arch of one of the vertebrae not fusing together so that the spine is split in two. The spinal cord may protrude through this gap. The symptoms of spina bifida may include paralysis of the legs, incontinence and mental disability as a result of hydrocephalus, which is commonly associated with spina bifida. Children with spina bifida are very prone to urinary infections, which may cause unexpected lack of attention or interest, vomiting and fever.

What is spina bifida?

**What is
hydrocephalus?**

Hydrocephalus may occur on its own or in association with spina bifida. It may be present at birth or develop later. In early life the main symptom is an enlarged head. When it occurs in older children and adults, it causes headaches, vomiting, fits or progressive paralysis. Hydrocephalus may be treated.

Many people with hydrocephalus and/or spina bifida have a shortened life span. A few live on into adulthood, when the additional problem of increasing weight heightens the risk of getting bed sores.

Early years services for children

Education underpins health and care in many ways as it provides people with information, helps them to acquire skills and knowledge and influences their values. Education influences people's attitudes and plays an important part in developing their identity, self-esteem and social skills. Formal education includes pre-school education such as nurseries and playgroups, which provide important learning opportunities for young children.

The delivery of any services for children should be based upon the following principles:

- Services should be delivered in partnership with parents.
- The needs and welfare of the children are paramount.
- All children have a right to play in a safe, supportive and stimulating environment.
- Services should take account of the needs of all children, whatever their gender, race, culture, language, disability or particular needs.
- Authorities should work to develop a universal service that does not stigmatise children. These services should be developed in partnership with the voluntary and private sectors so that parents have a wide and varied choice of services.

Services available for children under 8 years of age

Day nurseries (private, voluntary and local authority). There were over 6100 day nurseries providing about 194 000 places for children in 1988. Day nurseries look after under-fives for the length of the working day. A number are run by Social Services departments or education departments but voluntary groups, private companies or individuals also provide this facility.

Playgroups. The number of playgroups continues to fall each year. In 1988 there were 15 000 providing 3 840 000 places. Playgroups provide sessions of care for children aged between 3 and 5. Some groups may take children at the age of 2½ years. Playgroups aim to provide learning experiences through structured play in groups. Many of the groups are run with the involvement of parents on a self-help basis with one or two paid staff. A few playgroups are run by local authorities and some cater for children with special needs. Many playgroup sessions last for a morning or afternoon.

Childminders. A total of 98 000 registered childminders provide 365 000 places for children. Childminders look after children of all ages during the working day. Parents and childminders arrange payment between themselves.

Out-of-school clubs. Out-of-school clubs provide sessional support for children before and after school. Holiday schemes provide care all day during school holidays.

Family centres. Family centres provide a range of facilities for children such as play sessions, toy libraries and out-of-school activities. They also provide support for adults such as advice or therapy. These centres can be attended by children of any age and their families. Many such centres are run by the Family Welfare Society or Dr Barnardos – both are voluntary organisations.

How do the health, social care and early years services meet the needs of elderly people?

Improving standards of living and social and medical advances have meant that many more people are living longer. This, combined with a rise in birth and child survival rates earlier in the 20th century, has resulted in a higher proportion of older people in the population. A man born in 1901 could expect to live for an average of 45 years and a woman for nearly 50 years. It is estimated that a woman born in 2001 can expect to live for 80 years and a man for 75 years. Life expectancy is currently increasing by about two years every decade. The average child born in 1994 will live about 25 years longer than a child born in 1901.

The number of people over 85 continues to grow at a dramatic rate. However, many older people are 'young' in body and mind and their health needs vary. The health needs of people in their 60s are different from those of people over 85. The majority of older people require no care or require care only occasionally.

As more people are living longer they become dependent on others for help for longer periods than in the past. The total number of people in the UK over 65 years of age has risen from 2 879 000 in 1911 to 10 668 000 in 1996, with approximately twice as many women in this group as men. The number of the elderly will continue to increase over the next few decades to 11.8 million in 2010 and 14 million in 2021 – an increase that will add considerably to the pressures on the health and social care services.

The profile of the elderly population is also changing. The most significant change is the increase in the number of the 'old old' – those

people retire every day and their pension should pay for comfortable housing, adequate food, fuel and lighting and a good supply of warm clothes. More and more elderly people have only the state pension and other benefits to live on. Nearly half of all benefits paid in 1990s were accounted for by payments to this group.

You can use Activity 6 to provide evidence for Key Skills Communications C2.1b

---

Activity 6

Visit some elderly people who are living in their own homes. If they are willing, discuss with them what they spend their income on.

Give a short presentation to your class on your findings.

Support for people who use health, social care and early years services

Older adults have the right to independence and privacy and should have opportunities to participate in the life of their local communities, but for many these rights are not respected. This can be a particular problem when people are cared for in residential or day care.

Every person has access to health and social care services but many may not know of their rights because they cannot read or speak English. Most health and social care organisations have published pamphlets and leaflets describing their services and how people can use them – the Patient's Charter, for instance (this is discussed in more detail later in this unit). These sources of information are often published in languages other than English, such as Chinese and Gujarati. Many hospitals have appointed workers to act for patients and take up any complaints they may have. They also provide interpreters to help clients whose first language is not English.

Many organisations are dedicated to supporting clients in receiving adequate services. For example, Mencap provides help, support and advice for those with learning difficulties, while the MS Society does the same for those suffering from multiple sclerosis. Sources of help and support can also be obtained from a Citizen's Advice Bureau, local council advice officers and the local Community Health Council.

The main jobs in the health, social care and early years services

Health care staff

Approximately 950 000 people were employed in the NHS hospital and community services in 1988. Of these staff, 68% were direct care workers and 32% were management and support staff. Numbers had fallen to 804 000 in 1997.

NHS staff 1997

Nurses, midwives and health visitors	508 000
Doctors and dentists	57 000
Administration	167 000
Support staff	82 000

Direct care workers	**Indirect care workers**
Social worker	Medical receptionist
Home care assistant (home help)	Cleaner
Meals-on-wheels staff	Hospital porter
Hospital doctor	Hospital reception staff
Hospital nurse	Hospital manager
General practitioner	Security staff
Practice nurse	GP health centre manager
District nurse	Clerical staff
Health visitor	
Midwife	
School nurse	
Community psychiatric nurse	
Radiographer	
Physiotherapist	
Occupational therapist	
Speech therapist	
Chiropodist	
Nursery nurse	

Social workers

Social care can be divided into:

- community care
- residential care
- domiciliary and day care.

Working in both areas are qualified social workers who have obtained a qualification covering all areas of social work, although they may specialise in one area later. The qualification most of them have is the Certificate of Qualification in Social Work (CQSW). However, recent changes to training have involved the development of a new Diploma in Social Work (DipSW), replacing both the CQSW and the Certificate in Social Service (CSS). This latter (CSS) was a professional qualification that was undertaken mainly by residential and day care and domiciliary staff.

Field social workers provide support to all types of client: individuals and families, both in the community and in hospital (hospital social workers). The social worker provides social rehabilitation and community services, specialising in child care work, helping elderly people or working with people suffering from mental illness. About £207 million was spent on field social workers by local authorities in 1997.

The role of the social worker is to assess a client's and carer's needs and to organise, with other professionals, services to meet those individual needs. Social workers may be able to offer a wide range of services; access to these services will depend on where the client lives.

Key worker
Social worker

Key client groups
All client groups

Activity 7

Mrs MacCarty is 90 years old and lives with her sister of 70. She has just had a bad fall and has broken her right arm

a List the SSD practitioners who might offer support to Mrs MacCarty and her sister.
b Discuss what services these practitioners could offer her to allow both of them to stay in their own home. You may need to do some further research on your own to complete this exercise.

Home care assistants

A number of home care staff provide emotional, social and practical support to clients living in their own homes in the community. Local authorities have a duty (this means they must provide this service) to provide home helps (now called home care assistants or home carers). Many home care assistants work for private organisations and offer people a service in their own homes for a fee. The private sector now provides 44% of home care services, compared to just 2% in 1992.

Working mostly with older people, they carry out such tasks as simple cleaning, lighting fires, shopping, cooking and basic personal tasks. They also write letters and provide social support. Most of their work is concerned with supporting elderly people but they do also work with people with physical disabilities and families with young children. In 1998 over 470 000 households in England were supplied with a home help.

Key worker
Home care assistant

Key client groups
Older people and people with disabilities

Meals-on-wheels staff

This service is becoming increasingly important as more and more elderly dependent people choose to live in their own homes. About 33 million meals are provided every year in England to people in their own homes. This service is provided by the local authority in many areas, but it is still also offered by voluntary agencies such as the Women's Royal Voluntary Service or the Women's Institute in rural areas. Over 760 000 meals-on-wheels were provided in 1998 to people in their own homes. The private sector now provides 41% of meals to people in their own homes and 65% of meals to luncheon clubs.

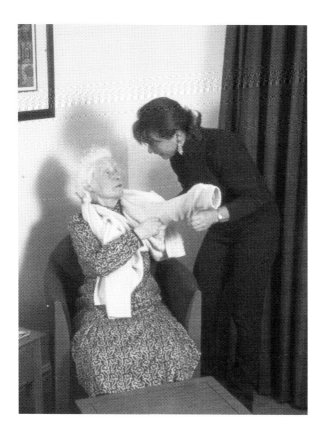

A home care assistant

Meals-on-wheels is one of the most important forms of community support for elderly people in their own homes. It makes a contribution to their nutritional needs and is often the only social contact that an elderly person has during the week. The service can also improve the morale of elderly people. As the elderly are most susceptible to hypothermia, the daily visit of meals-on-wheels staff can provide a check that all is well.

Key worker   **Key client groups**
Meals-on-wheels staff   Older people

Activity 8

a Find out who runs the meals-on-wheels service in your locality.
b Arrange to interview the organiser. Find out the kinds of client that the service supports and the types of meal delivered.

Hospital doctors

The care provided by the NHS means that anyone in Britain can visit their GP whenever they feel ill. In an average year, over 9.7 million referrals were made to hospitals for treatment and 11.2 million were treated by the accident and emergency services. Surgeons carried out over 3.5 million operations. In hospital, patients are looked after by teams of doctors who specialise in particular areas, such as paediatrics (children), obstetrics (pregnancy and childbirth) and geriatrics (elderly people). The role of the doctors is to:

- diagnose – find out what is wrong with the patient
- prescribe – decide on the treatment to help the patient
- monitor – review the condition of the patient and change the treatment if necessary.

Patients are usually referred to hospital doctors by their GPs.

Hospital doctors are supported by other professionals, such as nurses, physiotherapists and social workers – the multidisciplinary team (see page 8). The senior doctors on the team may be referred to as specialists or consultants or the Medical Director.

Key worker   **Key client groups**
Hospital doctor   All client groups

Hospital nurses

Most nurses are to be found working in hospitals alongside doctors. There are two levels of personnel in the nursing team currently employed in the NHS: registered general nurses (RGNs) and health care assistants (HCAs), who support the RGNs. There are still many state enrolled nurses (SENs), but initial training has ended and so in future all nurses will be at RGN level.

Key worker   **Key client groups**
Hospital nurse   All client groups

General practitioners (GPs)

GPs are just one part of the front line of the NHS and work in that part of the service called 'primary care'. Services offered by GPs are free to patients, although there are flat charges for some patients. Children, elderly people and those on low incomes receive prescriptions free.

Most people select their own general practitioner when they are over 16 years old, from the list of GPs kept by the District Health Authority. Most GPs now work together with others in group practices. Within the group practice are GPs, receptionists, administrative staff and probably a **practice nurse** and a social worker employed by the practice. Health visitors may also be based in GP practices.

Key worker   **Key client groups**
GP   All client groups

Practice nurses

The practice nurse is usually employed directly by a GP practice, where most of their work is carried out. The practice nurse carries out such routine tasks as dressings, urine tests and injections. The practice nurse may run 'well woman' and 'well man' clinics and may also offer a counselling service to patients and relatives. At present there are approximately 4000 practice nurses.

Key worker
Practice nurse

Key client groups
All client groups

District nurses

District Health Authorities have a responsibility to provide nurses to assist with treatment in a patient's home. There are approximately 20 000 district nurses currently employed, providing support and nursing care for acute and chronic patients of all ages, but predominantly for elderly people in their own homes. They also provide the link between hospitals and the primary health care team by referring patients to other carers and services.

Key worker
District nurse

Key client groups
Older people

Health visitors

There are about 13 000 practising health visitors in England, Wales and Scotland. The health visitor is an RGN with postgraduate training and the Health Visitor's Certificate. The role of the health visitor is in the area of health education, prevention of illness and promotion of health in antenatal classes and health clinics, monitoring the development of children and with patients in their own homes. The health visitor also has a large part to play in the community care of the elderly.

Key worker
Health visitor

Key client groups
Children and older people

Midwives

Midwives are independent, professional nurses in their own right. They are responsible for supervising antenatal and postnatal care of all women, whether they have their baby in hospital or in their own homes. They look after the mother and baby for 10 days after birth. They may be based in the community or in a hospital. There are approximately 5000 midwives working in the community.

Key worker
Midwife

Key client groups
Expectant mothers, and mother and baby for 10 days after birth

School nurses

The school nurse promotes positive attitudes to health within the education system. She gives advice on health matters to school staff and looks after the children, carrying out screening checks and giving advice about such matters as immunisation. Fewer and fewer school nurses are being employed.

Key worker
School nurse

Key client groups
School children

Community psychiatric nurses

What do the initials CPN stand for?

Community psychiatric nurses (CPNs) and the community-based mental handicap nurses (RNMHs) provide continuing care and support for people who may have been receiving long-term hospital care and who are now returning to life in the community. The link between health and social care is through social workers and community-based nurses.

Key worker
Community psychiatric nurse

Key client groups
People who suffer from psychiatric or learning disabilities

Other health professionals

While the main, face-to-face delivery of care is carried out by nurses and doctors, there is a large range of professions allied to medicine.

Radiographers

Diagnostic radiographers use X-rays and ultrasound to visualise bones and internal organs to check for abnormalities. Therapeutic radiographers use ionising radiation (such as X-rays and gamma rays) to destroy tissues and thus help the patient. In particular, such treatments are used on a wide range of cancers.

In both cases the radiographer works as a technician, instructed by a radiologist. The radiologist is a specialist doctor who, for example, interprets X-ray pictures and produces reports for the doctor requesting the X-ray.

Key worker
Radiographer

Key client groups
All client groups

Physiotherapists

Physiotherapists have an important role in improving the mobility of patients, using supportive and manipulative exercises to develop muscles for movement. Physiotherapists improve the health and function of clients through simple corrective exercises. They often use equipment such as infrared and ultrasound machines. They work in co-operation with doctors in planning the physiotherapy programmes. There are now approximately 9500 physiotherapists working in the NHS. A number work in private practice.

Key worker
Physiotherapist

Key client groups
Clients needing rehabilitation after physical injury or illness

Occupational therapists

Over 4500 occupational therapists (OTs) work in the NHS to treat illness, both mental and physical, with activity. A large part of their work is with clients or patients suffering from a physical or learning difficulty. They work on a one-to-one basis, with groups and with recreational activities. The aim is to rehabilitate the client and teach them basic living skills. Many OTs work in the community and are also employed by Social Services departments, offering advice on aids and adaptations for daily living.

What do the initials OT stand for?

Key worker
Occupational therapist

Key client groups
People with physical or learning disabilities

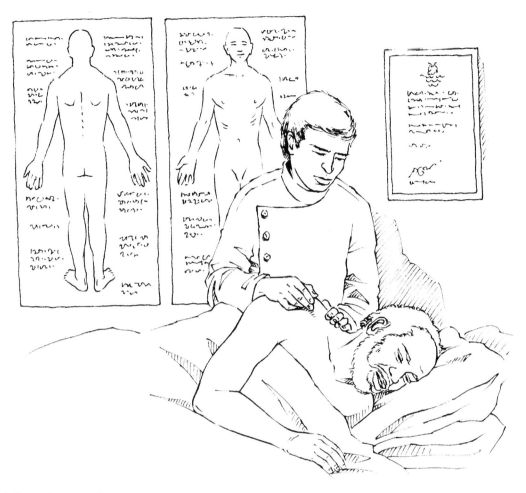

A physiotherapist at work

Speech therapists

Speech therapists help people with speech disorders. These range from children with delayed speech development to older people recovering from strokes. Most of their work, however, is with children.

Key worker
Speech therapist

Key client groups
Older people and children

Chiropodists

Chiropodists work with all client groups, dealing with such complaints as corns, ingrown toenails and hammer toes. Over 1 million chiropody sessions are carried out each year and the majority of people who receive this service are 65 or over.

Key worker
Chiropodist

Key client groups
Older people

Specialist support workers with children

The Children Act 1989 imposed duties on local authorities to provide daycare for children in need under 5 years of age. Day nurseries for children between 6 months and 5 years old are staffed by workers with qualifications in child care. The special skills required for this type of care are recognised. Nursery nurses have either a National Nursery Examinations Board (NNEB) qualification or the Edexcel National Diploma or Certificate in Childhood Studies (Nursery Nursing). They may also have either the NVQ qualification, the CACHE Diploma or the Edexcel (BTEC) Higher National Diploma in Childhood Studies.

National Vocational Qualifications (NVQs) in health and social care

In recent years the UK government has encouraged training for National Vocational Qualifications (NVQs). At the moment, these qualifications in health and social care mainly affect those working in the hospital, residential, day or home care fields. NVQs rely on the candidates demonstrating that they are competent to do the job for which they are being assessed. Thus in many areas of social care that were traditionally staffed by untrained, unqualified people there are now qualifications and recognition of the skills of the work force.

1.2 The care value base

Much of our interpersonal interaction is guided by our personal values and attitudes. What we think is right and true affects the way we behave. Many of the ideas and assumptions we have are based on what we were told as children and later on what we have seen and heard on television or read about. Sometimes our own prejudices or personal fears and values are more subtle but still significantly affect how we relate to people.

Inevitably, the caring role can give rise to difficult situations for both client and carer. Some of the more relevant situations are described below.

Working with people is seldom an easy option. You may often feel:

- overworked, so that you do not have the energy to listen to clients
- that your personal problems are affecting your work and attitude towards clients
- tired and impatient
- immature and unable to understand a client's problem
- that you have difficulty in forming relationships with clients or colleagues

- worried because the demands of your job are excessive
- overwhelmed with paperwork
- not trained enough for the demands of the job.

Perhaps you can think of other issues that might arise?

Sometimes you may feel overwhelmed by the responsibilities and tasks you are expected to carry out. It is at times like this, when you are under stress, that it is most important that you remember and work with the care values in mind. Care values are principles, standards or qualities considered worthwhile or desirable by the care profession. An individual's attitudes and values can be observed in their behaviour. Although it is difficult to change attitudes, and hence values, some vocations, such as health and social care, require a great deal of attention to be paid to them.

The social care value base

Social care values address five elements:

- *Antidiscriminatory practice* with reference to culture, race, religion, sexual identity, age, gender, health status, etc.
- *Confidentiality* – clients have the right to say who should have access to personal data and care workers are responsible for respecting the wishes of the client.
- *Individual rights and choice* – clients' choice, preferences and wishes must be respected.
- *Personal beliefs and identity* – each individual's own personal beliefs and preferences (religious, cultural, political, ethical and sexual) must be respected.
- *Effective communication* – listen to other individuals, promote effective communication in a variety of ways, consider language (verbal and non-verbal), understanding, environment, and social and cultural influences.

It is hoped that by stimulating thought and discussion, and exposing carers to a wide variety of situations, attitudes may be developed that are consistent with this value base.

The intention of having care values is to create equality for all individuals. Most professional carers are employed by agencies that have considerable power, and that also have responsibilities in law to others besides service users. While we emphasise the therapeutic, supportive and counselling roles of care workers, they are also responsible to the agency that they work for. A care worker may be better educated and therefore, by definition, possess more power through their position than their client. To counteract these processes the new Diploma in Social Work identifies values that are integral to competent social work practice. It states that social workers should:

- identify and question their own values and prejudices, and their implications for practice
- respect and value uniqueness and diversity, and recognise and build on strengths

- promote people's rights to choice, privacy, **confidentiality** and protection while recognising and addressing the complexities of competing rights and demands
- assist people to increase control of, and improve the quality of, their lives while recognising that control of behaviour will be required at times in order to protect children and adults from harm
- identify, analyse and take action to counter discrimination, racism, disadvantage, inequality and injustice, using strategies appropriate to role and context
- practise in a manner that does not stigmatise or disadvantage either individuals, groups or communities.

The social or health problems of some clients may create real dependency. To be thought of as anything other than fit, able and making a valuable contribution to society is to be stripped of power. Some care services inadvertently reinforce this problem in the way that they provide their services. Those who provide care services are not immune from the attitudes of the society into which they themselves have been socialised. They may have attitudes that reinforce many of the prejudices that society has about people who are different, for whatever reason. Care settings may mirror the effects of power on vulnerable individuals in both public and private settings.

Key Skills

You can use Activity 9 to provide evidence for Key Skills Communication C2.1a, C2.1b

---

Activity 9

Divide the class into five groups, each group choosing one of the five elements that make up the value base. Discuss in your group how your chosen element can be put into practice by those working in care settings, for example homes for the elderly, day centres for those with physical disabilities, clubs for people with learning difficulties. Make notes of your discussion and report back to the whole class.

Confidentiality – ethical issues in health and social care

This is a principle common to all health, social care and early years services. Before any information you have gained is shared with other people the client's permission must be obtained. If the reasons why you want to share the information are made clear to the client, then consent is more likely to be given.

We have mentioned confidentiality in the sense of betraying trust. If someone trusts you sufficiently to talk to you deeply about themselves or their problems, then that trust should never be broken. It is demeaning to the other person if you chat about them openly. It would also be very distressing to anyone who knew the other person. If you need help yourself because of what a client has told you, then you must go to the supervisor in private.

There are two levels of confidentiality. The first is that there are many things you need never speak about to anyone. If it is your task on placement to help an elderly man who has wet himself to change his trousers, you do the task and say nothing. It is unprofessional to moan on the bus about what a fuss it was. How would you feel if it was your father, or indeed, have you never been in an embarrassing situation yourself?

The second level is when someone is discussing an issue with you and you need to warn them that, if what they say cuts across legal boundaries or the rules of the establishment you are in, you will have to pass the information on. For example, if someone in a hostel was about to tell you that they sniffed glue, you would have to say that you would need to speak to someone more senior about it. If they had already told you, the rule would still apply. There are times when client confidentiality has to be limited.

Activity 10

a You are a social worker attempting to help a very disturbed and disruptive girl of 15. After many failures you eventually win her confidence, or appear to. During a casual conversation she implies, but does not say outright, that she has been having sex with a 17-year-old boy who has left school. What do you do?

b You are working in a home for children and a 14-year-old girl is very sharp with you one day. When you tackle her about it she gets very upset, apologises and says she needs to talk to you. She swears you to secrecy because she knows the rows and damage that will follow if her story is revealed. She tells you that her father has made sexual advances to her. She thinks she can cope and distance him – she says he is really kind to her and never forces her. She feels very mixed up. She isn't even sure if she has misinterpreted his attitude towards her. The last thing she wants is for the story to be known. She loves her mother and doesn't want her to be upset by this, particularly as her mother has been very ill. Her two younger brothers would also be badly affected by allegations. What do you do?

It may be helpful to discuss these situations with the whole group before moving on to the next exercise.

Individual rights – treat each person as an individual

Unless you treat each person as an individual you are likely to make assumptions about them – that is, you may make a judgement about them based on something you have seen or read. The judgement may be wrong but it affects your interaction with that person. The assumption grows to a stereotype – we make the person fit the image we have of them rather than accepting them for what they are. Stereotypes act as barriers to good communication. Good carers try to be aware of the stereotypes they may believe in, particularly when the person they are trying to help is from a different social class, from a different ethnic background or of the opposite gender. Here are some examples of how we can easily misjudge people and get the wrong message.

- *Judging on appearance*. 'The guy looked so punk I thought he was very threatening but he was really gentle when he worked with the toddlers.' *Day nursery assistant*

- *Judging age*. 'Old people don't care about their appearance so I don't bother if the hem of Doris's underskirt falls below her dress or Pop walks around with his fly undone.' *Care assistant in elderly persons' home*

- *Judging disabled people* – see the wheelchair and assume total immobility. 'I was really surprised when I pushed the wheelchair to the toilet block and she got up and walked to the toilet on her own.' *College tutor who has just had a disabled student join a course*

* *Judging academic ability to be the same as emotional and social ability.* 'Some of them are so slow you wouldn't think they'd be interested in anything romantic.' *Student working alongside some other students with learning difficulties*

By responding to people as individuals you are respecting who they are and what they want. You are giving them some scope to make a choice and exercise control.

An old people's home offering respite care or temporary care for elderly people while relatives have a break admitted a man from a Jewish background. The staff could have assumed that he wouldn't mind just eating like everyone else for his fortnight stay. They could have assumed that he was no longer practising his religion. They did, however, check his dietary requirements and took trouble to obtain the right Kosher food. This made a huge difference to his stay.

Activity 11

Making judgements – checking values

a As a group discussion, consider the following people and ask yourself how you would feel about helping them. Follow through by asking why you felt that way.

  i A lonely elderly person with financial problems and bad housing

  ii A mother of four who is depressed and has assaulted one of her children

  iii A group member who is absent from college because of emotional problems

  iv A teenage boy at a private school whose parents are rich but who himself has financial difficulties

►►

v A man suffering from depression after a driving accident in which someone was killed (the man had been drinking)

vi A man who is living rough, who smells and who pesters you for money.

Keynote: assumption → stereotype → prejudice → discrimination → denies individuality

Make a note in your file about your feelings and how they might link with assumptions and stereotyping.

b In your group discuss possible areas of stereotyping.

c Work out how stereotyping might lead to prejudice.

Gender

We are socialised into our gender roles from the minute we are born, by the colour of the blanket that is wrapped around us and the sorts of card that are sent to greet us.

Activity 12

Write down the gender that you think is best suited to the following occupations/careers. Your answers will help you in identifying any stereotypes you may hold:

a Nanny
b Nurse
c Engineer
d Domestic worker
e Builder
f Joiner
g Counsellor

h Footballer
i Car mechanic
j Financial adviser
k Electrician
l Plumber
m Caterer
n Councillor

Age

When did you last run a marathon? It is not only the aged who do not normally do this. Negative stereotyping about age highlights sickness, dependency and not being able to be sociable. Older people may be seen by others as retarded, slow or inefficient. If they show interest in sex this may be regarded as odd, funny or dirty.

Disability

Often, assumptions are made about disabled people's abilities that are based on misunderstanding. Access and opportunities are very significant to disabled people. If they are denied access to a building or the opportunity to do a job then they cannot demonstrate the capabilities they have. Similarly, some disabled people have experienced difficulties socially with access to nightclubs and other venues, on the tenuous pretext of increased fire risk. The more probable explanation is the negative stereotyping of nightclub managers that disabled people are not 'good' people to have around – they weaken the 'good time' image of the place.

The effects of discrimination

The possible effects of discrimination are so pervasive and wide-ranging that it is impossible to explain or describe them in depth or with accuracy. Reading novels, poems, watching films or television programmes and listening to personal experiences can inform us about the possible effects of discrimination.

Activity 13

Consider the physical, intellectual, emotional and social implications of discrimination for the following groups of people. Make a list of the groups and give examples of how discrimination may affect them. Some clues are provided.

a Women. Clues:
- *Physically* – may never achieve full physical potential because of traditional notions of weakness. Although it is illegal, women may still be barred from participating in particular sports. May be unlikely to gain employment in certain occupations. May be denied career or promotion opportunities because of their biological capacity to bear children.
- *Intellectually* – may be considered as intellectually less capable in some areas and therefore not given opportunities educationally: 'My father encouraged my brother but he didn't think it was worth educating a girl.'
- *Emotionally* – 'I wanted to apply for the promotion but I didn't feel it was right – the management are nearly all men. I should concentrate on things at home; my mother said it was wrong to leave the children and she's probably right.' 'I would like to learn French at evening classes but there is so much to do at home, what with the family, and Grandad needs more help now.'
- *Socially* – the traditional roles of women are often underpaid and undervalued. 'Anyone can look after children.' 'Nobody wants to spend the day cooking and doing housework.'

Key Skills

You can use Activity 13 to provide evidence for Key Skills Communication C2.3

▶▶

37

b Ethnic minority group members. Clues:
- *Physically* – may be discriminated against in terms of access to health care – the health service runs mainly on white, middle-class systems and culture.
- *Intellectually* – in classrooms, racist tensions among staff and pupils can affect educational progress and intellectual development.
- *Emotionally* – may have feelings of being different or singled out, like the black boy who wanted to wash his hands white.
- *Socially* – the unemployment level for people from ethnic minorities is significantly higher than for white people. There are still few people from ethnic minorities in senior positions in professional occupations. Similarly, they have encountered racism in terms of housing, lodgings and temporary accommodation. It is only relatively recently that black footballers have played in league teams and it is very rare for people from Asian racial groups to do so.

c Disabled people. Clues:
- *Physically* – good access often denied so life becomes more difficult.
- *Intellectually* – may be regarded as intellectually weak even if their disability is physical.
- *Emotionally* – dependence may have been encouraged from childhood; this is usually well-intentioned but it creates a situation where the person feels dependent on others and fails to develop independence, even over matters like choice of clothes or hairstyle.
- *Socially* – disabled people may have been subtly dissuaded from visiting holiday centres, clubs, pubs and cinemas.

d Lesbian and gay people. Clues:
- *Physically* – may be subject to abuse and bullying.
- *Intellectually* – may be discriminated against in education by staff or pupils, which could affect intellectual progress.
- *Emotionally* – reactions to comments about being odd or different, general stigma and unkind responses may all combine to produce low self-esteem, isolation and withdrawal. Such negative emotions affect an individual's general outlook and world view.
- *Socially* – may be discriminated against with regard to jobs, promotion and even accommodation in, for example, shared housing or lodgings.

Personal belief, identity and dignity – non-judgemental attitude

Everyone has stereotypes to a certain extent. We make judgements about people in our minds so that we can interact with them. For example, if you met a young male wearing sports clothes you might assume that he enjoyed playing sport. If you met a teenage girl wearing trendy clothes you might assume that she liked listening to music and socialising. You might be very wrong in both cases, but the misjudgements are probably not damaging.

When is stereotyping damaging and when does stereotyping become discrimination? These are not easy questions to answer because there may only be a subtle difference between stereotyping that is helpful and stereotyping that is damaging to the other person. It is important that people who work in health, social care and early years services should have a **non-judgemental attitude**. Categorising people is not helpful when it leads you to assume that those who look or behave like the mental image you have of some class of person actually belong to that category. When people make assumptions like this we call it **prejudice**. It means someone has prejudged the other person or group – made up their minds beforehand. They have a personal bias, based on something they have heard or seen. This is confirmed and perpetuated by means of their responses to people and their interactions with them.

Look at these comments – you can understand that there is prejudice and unhelpful categorisation in them:

- A woman's place is in the home.
- People with AIDS have got what they deserve.
- Disabled people shouldn't have children – it's not fair to the children.
- Lesbians and gays shouldn't teach in schools.

Activity 14

a Look out for general statements in newspapers, magazines or on television that could lead to prejudice. Cut the statements or articles out or make a note of the television quotes and programme. Discuss with your colleagues how you would rewrite them.

b In a small group, discuss a particular area of prejudice – any prejudice will do, even against someone who supports a different football team from you. Discuss how you might overcome these prejudices.

Put yourself in the place of the person who 'suffers' from the prejudice. Ask yourself how it might feel to be disliked, ignored or bullied because you didn't have the same colour of skin or football scarf.

Examine your own prejudices – being aware of them is halfway to overcoming them.

Sometimes articles or programmes can take a particular slant that categorises people in a certain way as 'the Disabled' or 'the Elderly'. The article may be patronising (treating the people as if they were children) or give a lot of coverage to something a disabled person has achieved, however minor. This approach may have the effect of cutting disabled people off from mainstream society.

Antidiscriminatory practice – non-discriminatory attitude

While prejudice is what a person thinks, discrimination is what a person does – how they treat another person or group unfairly, based on their prejudice.

Forms of discrimination

Visual clues often guide our first impressions. We make judgements about people on the basis of what we see. Look at the list below and select the factors that you might be able to decide from sight:

- nationality
- marital status (married or single)
- sexual orientation (straight or gay)
- age
- social class or status
- religion
- criminal record
- disability/ability

- occupation
- politics
- problems with alcohol
- employed/unemployed
- race
- problems with drugs
- gender.

Why do you think that:

- Fat people might be more likely to receive negative treatment than slim people?
- Black people find it more difficult to secure accommodation than white people?
- Women who dress in a very masculine way may find it more difficult to succeed in a job application if interviewed by men?
- Teachers might devote less time to female pupils than male pupils in mixed classes?

Activity 15

Make your own list of possible areas of discrimination, using the clues in this section and others you can glean from class discussion. Check your own feelings about the areas you have listed. Why do you think people in the above list might be treated unfairly?

Language

On a cultural level, our language is peppered with both sexist and racist terms that are indirectly discriminatory. Often the words 'man', 'he', 'him' are used to refer to both genders.

Activity 16

Work out alternatives for:

- businessman
- manning
- man hours
- manpower
- man-made
- fireman
- to a man
- headmaster
- foreman
- chairman
- cameraman
- ice cream man
- salesman
- newsman
- dustman

Language and race

In the first part of the 20th century the terms 'Negro', 'coloured', etc. were commonly used. The development of black movements in the 1960s led to the use of the word 'black' as a good term so it has been kept and used.

Negative uses of the word 'black', which have come from a racist situation, such as 'working like a black', should be avoided. Several phrases are negatively associated with 'black', such as 'black magic', 'black sheep' or the use of the word 'black' to mean dirty. Such phrases need to be avoided.

Levels of discrimination

Prejudice or discrimination can arise at:

- an individual level, where people may have personal attitudes and beliefs that they use to prejudge other groups negatively
- an institutional level, where the systems and practices of an organisation exclude certain groups from access to resources – for example, if publicity about antenatal classes was not produced in community languages in a multiracial area, this could be seen as institutional racism
- a cultural level, where people have so absorbed values, beliefs and ideas that they don't challenge negative stereotypes in media images – these people accept racist or sexist remarks.

Behaviours indicating discrimination

These are obviously direct behaviours that are blatantly prejudiced, like using offensive language, denying people rights or being rude. A young black girl was sitting on the inside seat of a bus. Her white friend sitting beside her stood up to let an older woman sit down. The woman refused the seat, saying she would rather stand that sit next to 'one of them'. The black girl was the victim of *direct discrimination*.

Indirect discrimination is more subtle and less easy to report, but equally damaging. The director who has decided that he doesn't want to appoint a female assistant director may find ways of undermining her confidence so that she doesn't even feel she can apply for the post. She becomes the victim of indirect discrimination.

Devaluing someone by not taking them seriously or not respecting what they say is a form of indirect discrimination. For example, assuming that everyone has a Christian name is a form of indirect discrimination because many people are not Christian.

Activity 17

Racism is the belief that some 'races' are superior to others. Sometimes actions are clearly racist; at other times it is less easy to tell. Look at the situations below and decide whether:

▶▶

- the intention is not racist
- the method is not racist
- the effect is not racist.

a A housing department has a policy of spreading black tenants throughout its estates. The reasons given for this policy are to ensure that there is no discrimination against black applicants, leading to their being allocated to worse estates, and to encourage racial mixing.

b A company finds that it has more applicants for unskilled jobs than it has vacancies. In the past some of these jobs have been given to Asian workers who do not speak English fluently. They have been able to do the work satisfactorily and there haven't been any problems. Now that there are more applicants, the company have decided to ask all applicants to pass a test in basic written and spoken English before they can be offered a job.

c A company has a vacancy for a supervisor's post in a department where 60% of the workers are Asian. The supervisor's job includes explaining to the other workers what to do, filling in forms, report writing, etc. The company says all applicants for the job must pass a test to show that they have a good level of spoken and written English.

The answers are on page 70.

So it is necessary to check out not only what we intend but also our methods and the effects of our actions. Policies should also be checked out in this way.

Research shows that discrimination, both sexual and racial, is still strong and widespread despite legislation (see page 47).

Activity 18

Consider how much racial discrimination may affect the people making the comments below. Discuss your thoughts and record your answers.

a At school – intellectually, educationally
  i 'It's hard being the only black boy in the class. I'm noticed especially if I do anything wrong.' *Black 12-year-old boy*
  ii 'It's hopeless with these second-language speakers, they'll never get through the exam.' *English teacher*
  iii 'The PE staff keep asking me to play for this and that – they think because I'm black I'm really sporty, but I'm much more interested in history.' *Black 12-year-old boy*

▶▶

iv 'Sometimes I feel angry and resentful when I read about what white people did to blacks in the past and what still happens today. I don't feel like being co-operative at school.' *Black 14-year-old girl*

v 'People are just waking up to the fact that there are so few black people in senior positions in education, in commerce and industry. The unemployment rate among black youths is so much higher than for whites, considering the numbers in this population.' *Careers officer*

b In the community – socially

i 'Sometimes I know people view me differently because of the colour of my skin. The other day I was sitting on the bus. The person sitting next to me stood up to give an elderly lady the seat. The lady refused the seat, mumbling that she would rather stand than sit next to a Paki. I didn't realise how it had affected me until I arrived at school – I went to the toilets and had a good cry.' *Young Asian girl*

ii 'As jobs are scarce they've got to blame someone and we are the easiest target. Most of my family actually run their own businesses.' *Young Asian boy*

iii 'I saw a black family looking round the empty house up the road. That's all this neighbourhood needs.' *Mrs Snodgrass*

c Physically – in terms of health care

i 'We must have these leaflets about immunisation and surgery hours printed in community languages.' *Dr Smith, a GP.* 'Oh what's the point? They'll do their own thing anyhow – we've enough to do as it is.' *Dr Jones, Dr Smith's partner*

ii 'I find it so difficult to communicate sometimes with the Asian families. The babies usually thrive but I wish there were more Asian workers to relate to them more easily. I'm sure they'd open up more.' *Health visitor*

iii 'I can't understand why the Asian women will never look you directly in the eye when you're trying to make a point to them.' *Community psychiatric nurse*

iv 'Hospitals are such busy, bewildering places that it's easy to be put off unless you really need medical attention.' *White male outpatient*

How did you get on? Perhaps your discussion showed that it is easy for black people or minority groups to be nudged out of health care services and therefore discriminated against almost by chance without people noticing. Similarly in schools, attitudes are set and may create tensions before any learning takes place. In the community people are worried about employment and house prices and these fears are often directed against minority groups. Securing housing and employment therefore becomes more problematic for black people and, coupled with potential educational difficulties, such groups become disadvantaged through discrimination.

Activity 19

Ask the people in your group, 'Which would you rather be – male or female?' Ask someone to keep a record so that you can discuss their replies later. Then ask, 'If you, or your partner, were pregnant, which would you rather have – a boy or a girl?' Again keep a note.

Some research shows that more people actually want boys rather than girls. Why do you think this might be?

People evidently have images of boy or girl children in their minds and what those male or female roles mean in life.

Think about the moment a child is born – Is it all right? Is it a boy or girl? The pink or the blue blanket covers the little body. The cards arrive conveying good wishes for the bouncing boy or the sweet little daughter. Soon room decoration, clothes, toys, language, attitudes and responses all work to reinforce male or female roles. Later, books, films, television programmes and expectations of relatives, parents and teachers may further confirm these roles. There doesn't seem to be anything wrong with this, but consider the questions in Activity 20.

Activity 20

Tape your answers to the questions, or write them down and compare your answers with those of your colleagues.

a Why are there so few male nurses, secretaries, child minders, nursery teachers? What difficulties would a man have if he tried to do any of these jobs?
b What happens if a girl wants to follow a traditionally male-dominated career?
c Why are there so few women MPs?
d Why are there so few women in senior positions in industry?
e Why do we know so many more famous male authors and artists than female?
f In co-educational schools, who receives the greatest share of teacher attention?
g Who takes on the greatest amount of child-care and domestic responsibility?
h What are the problems for women who want to work and have a family?

When you answer these questions it becomes clear that, by prejudging people on the basis of gender, we are actually discriminating against them. We are not allowing them to develop in the way they wish to go. We stifle their choice and their ability to control. We stereotype them, we put them into a box in our minds, which may say, 'She is a woman who should take care of her family before she thinks about her career', or, 'He is a man who should have a job rather than being a house-husband.' This limits development and in some cases stops people aspiring to (trying to get) jobs or promotion.

Discrimination and disability

A similar process occurs in relation to mobility. It is easy to see a wheelchair or a white stick and categorise that person as being unable to cope. We may not even know what that person is capable of until further explanation.

Many disabled people feel that one of the worst aspects of being disabled is how other people perceive them. Very often it is assumed that disabled people cannot do things. For example, if someone is in a wheelchair there is a tendency for a speaker to address the person pushing the wheelchair rather than the person in the wheelchair. Of course, it is naive to suggest that a disabled person can do everything despite their disability, but if appropriate access, services and support are provided new avenues can be opened up. There is also a lot of evidence of disabled people achieving physical and academic feats that some able-bodied people would never dream of.

Since 1970 all public buildings must by law provide wheelchair access. Similarly, pathways, walkways and staircases should not restrict wheelchair users. In reality, there are still enormous difficulties in terms of access. This limits disabled people socially and in connection with employment. Similarly with housing, if a disabled person has an adapted home that they can manage, this increases their independence. If funds are low and they have to rely on other people then they are handicapped.

Sometimes a person's disability is not evident. They may have a mental health problem, but the same discriminatory practices may still occur. People may be refused jobs or promotion, or be disadvantaged socially or educationally because of attitudes formed by focusing on negative stereotypes.

What about you? Have there been times in your life when you have been unfairly treated because of your age, colour, social class, appearance or gender? How did you feel? Could you do anything about it?

Preventing and resisting discrimination

Personal prejudice

Most people have preferences. It is helpful if you are aware of your own preferences so that you can work on them to prevent prejudices. When you make decisions or choices you must try to avoid your own personal bias or preference affecting your judgement. This is particularly important when you are out on work placement. It is easy to like the attractive, well-dressed infant at the local nursery rather than some of the others, and to assume that this child is more intelligent and treat her/him accordingly. Some of the less obviously attractive pupils, however, may be equally or more capable, and deserve recognition.

For most people, first judgements are based on visual impressions. You may be able to recall times when you have judged somebody on sight and then later, when you have got to know them, realised how wrong your first impressions were. We categorise on sight. Research shows that:

- fat people are more likely to get negative treatment
- in mixed classes teachers devote more time to male pupils than to female pupils
- women who dress in a very masculine way are less likely to succeed in a job application if interviewed by men
- supervisors sum up young workers' behaviour in the first couple of weeks and don't change their opinions afterwards.

The first step must be to check your own prejudices and try to be aware of them in reacting in social care situations.

Working with children

If you are working with young children you can try to counteract stereotypical practices and language by:

- encouraging role reversal – the boys play in the Wendy house and the girls with Lego (is calling a playhouse the 'Wendy' house sexist?)
- selecting books and posters reflecting positive images of black children and non-sexist attitudes
- presenting toys and equipment in a non-sexist way

47

- avoiding sexist and racist language yourself and also monitoring children's conversations
- never saying things like 'Big boys don't cry' – it's probably better for the child to have a good bawl, male or female!
- being firm about racist actions or language from children – act quickly to report it to a member of staff if you don't feel that it is appropriate for you to deal with it
- not separating children on the basis of gender – grouping often sets up tensions and there is enough tension without creating more. Use birthdays or names beginning with particular letters
- pointing out role models if you can find any, such as a female garage mechanic, a male primary teacher or a male nurse.

At work

Most establishments have equal opportunities policies and **codes of practice** for dealing with racist remarks, attitudes or actions. Make sure you know who to report it to if you see or hear anything you regard as racist. If matters are dealt with promptly it is less likely that feelings will run high and escalate into violence.

If situations of violence do break out because of racism then obviously this is a matter for the police and the courts.

Legislation relating to discrimination

The Race Relations Act 1976

This Act makes racial discrimination illegal in public life. It says people can take action in circumstances involving employment, housing, education, provision of goods and services.

The Act outlines:

- direct discrimination – treating a person less favourably on the grounds of race
- indirect discrimination – applying certain criteria that work to the disadvantage of one category of person over another.

It also makes victimisation illegal – it is illegal to treat somebody unfairly for being involved in making a complaint about discrimination.

The Commission for Racial Equality can help in the preparation of Race Relations Act cases. The Citizen's Advice Bureau can also assist with these matters.

The Chronically Sick and Disabled Persons Act 1970

This Act attempts to reduce discrimination against disabled people. It instructs local authorities to provide services for disabled people and legislates (makes it law) that any new public buildings must provide access for disabled people.

The services that the Act recommended should be available to disabled people include:

- home care workers (home helps)
- meals-on-wheels
- adaptations to homes
- telephones
- aids to daily living
- occupation at home and at centres
- outings
- provision of transport.

The Act stated that local authorities had to know how many disabled people there were in their area.

The National Health Service Act 1977

This Act went on to make it a duty of the local authority to provide some home help services and recommends the provision of laundry services for people who need them.

The Disabled Persons Act 1986 (Services, Consultation and Representation)

This Act reinforces the need for assessment for disabled people and services. A disabled person or their representative may request an assessment.

The Sex Discrimination Act 1975

The Act applies to men and women. It states that it is unlawful to discriminate in the areas of recruitment, selection, promotion and training. It is also unlawful to treat a person less favourably because they are married. Like the Race Relations Act, it separates direct and indirect discrimination as well as victimisation.

The Equal Opportunities Commission and the Citizen's Advice Bureau can assist with complaints.

Equal Pay Act 1970

This Act should be considered alongside the Sex Discrimination Act. The Act was amended in 1983 to comply with the (then) EC law. The main point of the Act is that equal work must be rewarded with equal pay.

There is no legislation relating to religious discrimination in England and Wales. In Northern Ireland the Fair Employment Act 1989 covers this area.

Disabled Persons Act 1944 and 1988

Both Acts oblige companies employing more than 20 staff to employ 3% disabled people.

Employment Protection Act 1978

This deals with rights to guaranteed pay, medical suspension, time off work, maternity rights, sick pay and access to computerised data. Unions can be recognised at the discretion of the employer. Recognised unions can insist on equal opportunities policies and analysis of data to indicate how many black and white, male and female, disabled and non-disabled workers the company has.

The Disability Act 1995

This Act introduced new rights for people with disabilities in employment, transport, education and access to goods and services. Employers with 20 or more employees are required to treat people with a disability no less favourably than any other employee. Employers have to provide facilities to allow people with disabilities to be employed in the workplace.

Although laws against it do exist, discrimination continues because it takes a long time to change people's attitudes and ways of thinking. We can only challenge bad practice when we see it and try to promote as much good practice as possible.

Codes of practice and charters

A democratic and healthy society should provide a number of social rights and freedoms for its citizens. Expression of these rights, however, is often restricted by a variety of factors, including access to information. Information promotes health directly by giving people more power to influence their world. It helps them make decisions and choices about their health and gives them the ability to argue for changes. Information is essential for public involvement in the activities of organisations that affect people's lives, for example the NHS and local authorities.

The Citizen's Charter

The Citizen's Charter aims to raise the standard of public services and make them more responsive to the needs of the people who use those services. There are up to 40 charters published by individual public services under the auspices of the Citizen's Charter. These charters tell you about services, what standards you can expect and how to make a complaint. The following charters relate to health, social care and early years services.

- Parent's Charter – Department of Education
- Patient's Charter – Department of Health
- Council Tenant's Charter – Department of the Environment

The Patient's Charter

The Patient's Charter was introduced in 1992 setting out standards that a patient should expect of the NHS. The charter covers the whole NHS and focuses on areas of particular public concern, from right of access to personal respect, patient choice and the right to receive full and proper information about treatment and NHS services. The charter refers to the 'rights' of patients, but these 'rights' or standards are not guaranteed by law. In fact, the charter points out that they are 'not legal rights but major and specific standards which government looks to the NHS to achieve, as circumstances and resources allow'.

One of the new rights is for a patient's complaints to be investigated. The Department of Health said that complaints rose by at least 35% in 1993. However, many community health councils have stated that complaints more than doubled in 1993. Much of the information given by hospital and health authorities has not been found to be user-friendly and is often only provided on request. Many agree that the charter has made people feel good about complaining.

Existing standards specify the following:

- respect for privacy, dignity and religious and cultural beliefs
- availability of services to all, including people with special needs
- provision of information to relatives and friends of patients
- waiting time for ambulances (14 minutes in urban areas, 19 minutes in rural areas)
- waiting time for assessment in Accident and Emergency departments
- waiting time in outpatient departments
- what happens when an operation is cancelled
- a named member of nursing staff to be responsible for each patient.

Many health and social care organisations have published their own charter. Well over half of all GPs publish their own, and local health authorities set and publish their own standards.

Community Care Charter

Many local authorities have produced Community Care Charters. These charters describe what residents can expect from community care services in their area. They are usually developed in partnership with other agencies such as the health authority, housing departments and housing agencies.

A number of Social Services departments and local health authorities have jointly published Community Care Charters. Derbyshire County Council and its local health authorities are one example. The aims of its charter are:

- to inform people about the range of services available to assist them with community care needs and how they can gain access to them

  * to explain how the authorities decide if people qualify for a service
  * to highlight some of the standards which have been introduced and to explain how these standards are checked
  * to explain what people can do if things go wrong.

Northern Ireland and Wales also have their own charters, which relate to their services and particular organisations. The Northern Ireland Charter Standards for Community Services covers such areas as social services, hospital care, GP services and community nursing services.

Services for Children and Young People

Services for Children and Young People was first published in 1996. This charter sets out the rights and standards that apply in particular to children. This charter covers services for: the healthy child; babies and pre-school children; school children; young people; the sick child; the child with special needs; and the medical needs of children in local authority care.

Patient choice

People who use services are encouraged to exercise choice in choosing them. The government publishes national performance tables to show how hospitals are performing. It publishes such information as waiting times and how many operations of what kind have been performed in the past year. A maximum 18-month waiting period is specified for all inpatient treatment, a 12-month standard for coronary artery bypass grafts and a 26-week standard for patients to be seen by a consultant after referral by their GP.

The government expects to extend the amount of information published in the future so as to give users of the services more information on which to base their choices.

Codes of practice

Many organisations have now published codes of practice related to particular services such as home care (*Code of Practice,* United Kingdom Home Care Association 1990), residential care (*Home Life: A Code of Practice for Residential Care*, Social Care Association), and services for older people (*Home Help and Care: Rights, Charging and Reality*, Age Concern, 1992) or people with disabilities (*Living Options: Guidelines*, Advisory Group on Disability, 1985).

Almost all local authorities have published codes of practices indicating the standards that they have developed for individual services and giving information to users about what to do if they are dissatisfied about any aspect of the service.

For example, one local Social Services department has laid down six key principles that must be applied in homes for the elderly:

- privacy
- dignity
- independence
- choice
- rights
- fulfilment.

These codes of practice mean that any person admitted to residential care will have a right to privacy and confidentiality. The admission to residential care should not mean they lose their dignity; they should have a right to retain their independence and exercise choice. It is expected that residents will be given written information on these principles and how they are implemented in the particular home. The management should ensure that residents can have a key to their rooms and be able to lock their doors, that staff knock on bedroom doors and wait to be invited in and that people can retain their own personal clothes.

1.3 Skills needed by people working in health, social care and early years services

Interpersonal style

Interpersonal style is something we all have. Effective carers must explore their style and be familiar with it. In this way they will have greater awareness of the impact they make on others, have knowledge of, and be prepared to confront negative aspects of their style, and have clarified their value system.

Activity 21

This exercise will help you explore your attitudes and identify your interpersonal style.

a Complete the following sentences – don't spend a lot of time on them. Do it relatively quickly. Let the sentence act as a stimulus and put down whatever arises naturally.
   1. One thing I really like about myself is . . .
   2. I dislike people who . . .
   3. When people ignore me I . . .
   4. When someone praises me I . . .
   5. When I relate to people I . . .
   6. Those who really know me . . .
   7. My moods . . .
   8. I am at my best with people when . . .
   9. When I am in a group of strangers I . . .

10. I feel lonely when . . .
11. I envy . . .
12. I think I have hurt others by . . .
13. Those who don't know me well . . .
14. What I am really looking for in my relationships is . . .
15. I get hurt when . . .
16. I like people who . . .
17. What I feel most guilty about in relationships is . . .
18. Few people know that I . . .
19. When I think about intimacy . . .
20. One thing I really dislike about myself is . . .
21. I get angry with . . .
22. One thing that makes me nervous with people is . . .
23. When I really feel good about myself I . . .
24. When others put me down I . . .
25. When I like someone who doesn't feel the same about me I . . .
26. I feel awkward with others when . . .
27. I feel let down when . . .
28. In relationships what I run away from most is . . .
29. I hate people to see that I am . . .
30. What makes me really happy is . . .

b Did any of these questions give you a problem? If so, which?
c Which questions did you find hardest to answer? Why?
d Which question(s) were easiest to answer? Why?
e Would you like to add any other question? What?

Discuss your responses with your class colleagues.

Observation

While on placement it is useful to take the opportunity to observe how other workers interact with people and learn from them. Really, there is hardly a minute that cannot be used to gain some knowledge.

Use your observation skills also to help you to respond effectively to people:

- Is the person happy, sad, dejected?
- What is the person's attitude to other people and to his or her surroundings?
- Is the person anxious or tense?
- Can the person see?
- Can the person hear?
- Can the person talk or is signing used?

Listening

Listen actively. Get ready to listen. Make the shift from speaker to listener a complete one.

You must really focus and try to remember what the person has said. A good listener hears the content of what the speaker says and the intent – what the person means.

Activity 22

In pairs, allow one person to talk about a topic of his/her own choice for 3 minutes. The partner must listen actively and then report back to the main group what the other has said. Use a different topic to do the exercise the other way round.

Suggestions: My life to date, This past year, My kind of music, I enjoy doing . . ., I enjoyed my holiday in . . .

At an appropriate moment, you can check with the person whether you have understood everything by recalling what they have said. Don't interrupt them abruptly or ask too many questions otherwise it will be frustrating for the person trying to talk. This is called reflective listening. This reassures you that you have the right message and underlines to the other person the fact that you are listening. People are far more likely to open up to you and tell you what they are feeling if you are genuinely interested in them and this interest is shown by your reactions.

Reflective listening is sometimes called 'mirroring' – you mirror back to the person the content of what they have said. You need to concentrate to do this. As you become more skilled you will also be able to match the mood of the person by reflecting their feelings.

Activity 23

In groups of three, one person should explain a problem while one person listens and reflects by facial expression what the first person is feeling. The third person observes to see how accurately the listener is reflecting the feeling and writes a brief report to be kept as evidence.

Take it in turns to be the speaker, the listener and the observer.

A key to understanding emotions is to describe them! It can be helpful to suggest a particular word to the person that may describe their feelings. This means building up your language skills. Sometimes you need to put what has been said into your own words.

Activity 24

List as many words you can think of which describe the following emotions:

happiness   depression
anger   inferiority
shyness   irritation
grief   fear
anxiety

Be on the look-out, in your reading and viewing, for new adjectives to describe emotions.

Activity 25

In small groups, think of some responses which might be made to the following people:

a a friend who has had her purse, containing £60, stolen
b a teenager who had just failed her driving test
c a young man who has just been rejected for nurse training
d a mother whose child has been seriously injured in a road accident.

Ask others in the group to comment on your responses.

How we can use empathy to help people

As you listen actively and try to reflect back to the person their feelings and what they say, you will gradually move towards empathy. That is, you will be able to put yourself in the other person's position. You need to empathise in order to be able to help the person effectively.

Silence is golden . . .

We have so far emphasised the importance of listening, but sometimes people may just need a little space to be quiet. They need moments to pause, to regain themselves, to think of the words they need. It is not always easy to express feelings because it may be painful or embarrassing and there may be silence. Try to use the silence; try not to be tense about it. Even skilled counsellors can find silences difficult to handle. You may eventually be able to question gently.

Asking questions

There are more questions than answers . . .

Good questioning techniques can really improve your communication skills.

Some questions can be described as closed questions. That is, they can be answered very simply and don't give the person much opportunity to talk. Open questions, on the other hand, give the person more scope for talk. For example, you might ask a friend, 'Did you have a good time last night?' She could reply 'Yes' or 'No' or 'Not really' but if you asked, 'How did it go last night?' she might be awkward and say 'OK' but she is more likely to give you a fuller answer.

Although it is important to ask questions to clarify the situation or the problem, avoid asking too many. Otherwise, the person will feel burdened and unable to talk freely.

Avoid over-burdening the client with questions

Also avoid:

  telling the person, 'Don't worry – you'll soon forget it.' This puts the problem down – it makes it seem small. To the person the problem is big. S/he doesn't want to have it dismissed, s/he wants it talked through.

  telling the person what to do directly. There may be a course of action that is appropriate but the person should try and arrive at the decision themselves. You cannot dictate the perfect path through a tricky maze. The person has to arrive themselves, possibly with your help. For example, a friend of yours may have been seeing someone whom you are sure has little real consideration for her. The friend may ask your advice about ending the relationship. You could be tempted to say immediately, 'Ditch him. He's only using you', but it would be more effective to ask the friend questions about examples of his considerateness or consideration of her. This way she may gradually build up a picture and realise for herself that it isn't worth continuing the relationship.

being loud and overbearing. Obviously, if people have a hearing loss you have to speak up, but generally people appreciate a tone that's easy to listen to.

rushing to get it over with – you may be in a desperate hurry for a genuine reason and in this case you may have to ask to see the person at another time. Usually, however, it is best to go at the pace of the person you are talking to. Sometimes they can become 'locked' in a negative phase or keep going over the same point and you may have to question to move them on a little.

shifting the emphasis from the person to yourself and starting to recount your own experiences. Your client doesn't want to know your problems.

diagnosing 'what your problem is . . .'. By telling someone what their problem or need is you are putting your interpretation on it. It is only the problem as you see it, and not necessarily the whole problem or the problem as it affects their life. You are putting a value or a judgement on the person and the situation they are in. Again you may have it all wrong.

If you can, prepare questions in advance but don't be thrown if it doesn't work out the way you anticipate.

It may be that someone is reluctant to talk to you for a number of reasons or, having started to talk, dries up and cannot continue. You may help by asking open questions in relation to the subject and then some more specific closed questions to help you probe a little further. A lot depends on your understanding of the situation. If you feel a question might be too direct then make a suggestion (a prompt), but be careful – substituting words or giving ideas can be difficult. You can easily distance the person with the wrong suggestion.

Key Skills

You can use
Activity 26 to
provide evidence
for Key Skills
Communications
C2.1a

Activity 26

In small groups work out how you might respond to the following situations – what you might say or ask.

a You are working in an infant school and a child becomes upset because she cannot do her maths work.

b You are working in an infant school and a child refuses to do the art activity you have been asked to supervise. He says he is hopeless at art and he hates it.

c A member of your college group is finding her placement difficult and tells you that she isn't going to go the next day.

d You are working with a group of 16-year-old special needs students. They are having an aerobics session. Two of the students are finding it difficult to keep up with the others

e You are in a junior school on the day that the school football team is selected. Some boys are inevitably disappointed.

f You are working in a nursery where there are some children whose first language is not English. You hear one child saying, 'I'm not playing with Naseem because she doesn't talk proper.'

1.4 Basic communication skills needed by people working in health, social care and early years services

One of the most likely reasons why you chose to do this particular course is that you are interested in people. You may be the sort of person friends contact to talk over problems. You may have appreciated someone else listening to you to help you out. Your interest in people and in helping is a great advantage in health and social care situations, when you may be expected to give clients support.

You will probably be part of a team helping to provide this support, but your part is as important as that of anyone else. You may be able to think of examples when you have been in hospital or in a strange situation yourself and you have been glad of someone's warmth and friendliness towards you. That person may not have been the most highly paid or the most powerful in the establishment but they were of enormous significance to you.

What are the best ways of supporting people? How can good communication affect you and your relationships?

Just as people have physical needs – such as for food, sleep and warmth – and it is necessary to satisfy these needs, they also have emotional needs – the need to be liked, to be loved, to be wanted and respected or to be thought special.

Often, physical needs are direct, easy to see and in many cases easy to satisfy. Emotional needs, however, are more tricky to see and satisfy. And perhaps because they are less obvious and more difficult, carers can become preoccupied with physical tasks and fail to pick up on emotional needs. So try not to fall into the trap of providing physical care only. People have feelings, and feelings matter.

It can be considered a privilege if someone relates to you sufficiently well to 'open up' and talk to you. Their trust in you should not be taken lightly. You may need to refer to someone more senior than yourself for help, but you should never use the person as a conversation point within the establishment or outside.

Be worthy of the trust you have gained from your client. Be discreet but seek help when necessary – either for the client or for yourself – if you feel burdened by what has been said.

The importance of communication in delivering services to people

The fact that it is extremely difficult not to communicate shows how important communication is. At a fun level, see how long you can manage without communication! On a more serious note, think how hard it is for those in solitary confinement. Our instinct is to communicate with others because relationships hinge on communication, and without relationships living would be mere existence.

We tend to think of communication as speaking, but there are many ways to impart meaning or messages to others. It isn't just what we say that creates impressions but also how we express the words, what we wear, how we stand, look, behave, listen and respond. Sometimes we may give messages we don't intend.

How we develop communication skills

We all know how satisfying relationships can be and also how damaging. Some people can become lonely, unhappy and even mentally ill because they are unable, sometimes through no fault of their own, to establish and maintain social relationships. So one reason why it is important to communicate is because communication is part of a basic drive for us to form relationships.

As we form relationships we are actually affirming and presenting some aspect of ourselves. It is through relationships, and therefore through communication, that we express who we are, what we think, feel, know and want. Part of the process of expressing these things actually helps us to identify them. Sometimes it is difficult to know what we think, feel or want – when we can express it, then we know.

Communication is necessary to develop our sense of self and confirm what we are. On a practical level it helps us to cope with the demands of every day. Danger signs, warnings, notices of information for work and pleasure all form part of the significance of communication. Most of our learning, knowledge and, therefore, control is communicated to us.

On an emotional level expressions of affection, pleasure, anger, disappointment define, and often relieve, the intensity of the emotion. To talk about feelings helps us and those we support to come to terms with them. Children and adults who can't express emotion for whatever reason may experience great frustration and look for other ways to vent their feelings.

Communication is important because it helps us to:

- live our lives practically
- develop psychologically and intellectually
- express ourselves emotionally
- form relationships socially.

Activity 27

a Make a note of people who may have communication difficulties (think about sensory disabilities, mental health and social or relationship problems).
b Brainstorm how the communication barrier may affect the individual:
- practically, during their everyday lives
- educationally – at school
- emotionally – in terms of their feelings
- socially – in terms of relationships with others.

Key Skills

You can use Activity 27 to provide evidence for Key Skills Communication C2.1a

There are a number of skills that will help you to communicate effectively with other people:

taking opportunities to start conversations
observing
listening actively and reflectively
showing empathy
knowing when to keep quiet
knowing how to 'read' and use **non-verbal communication**, such as facial expressions, use of eye contact and posture
knowing how to ask questions
respecting people as individuals.

Take opportunities

Your confidence will grow as you gain more experience. Sometimes it is difficult when you first arrive at a placement to introduce yourself, to take the initiative to talk to someone, to sit down in a staff room, to ask where something is or check out something you don't understand.

A first step to relating to individuals is to remember their names. Listening to what they say and using this to help your conversation the next time you meet makes for positive interaction.

You may develop ways of remembering names. On placement you may see names on rooms or in school registers that you can memorise.

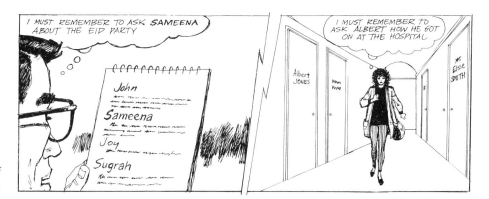

You may develop ways of remembering names

Activity 28

Role play the following situations. Organise a small group to be your 'supporting cast'.

a Your first visit to a home for elderly people where you are going to work for a placement exercise.
b Lunch time in an infant school. You are sitting next to the headteacher.
c You are working on a craft activity with a small group of 6-year-olds.
d You are accompanying a teacher and a small group of disabled children around the age of 7 on a visit to a farm.
e You are working in a playgroup and one group of children is baking some biscuits.
f Produce a list of good conversational strategies, which people could use in these situations.

After each role play, stop and discuss the exercise within your group. Were the conversation topics realistic? Did the conversation falter or dry up? Do you need to think more about your language?

Write a brief record of the exercise as evidence for your file. Note down where you need to improve.

How communication helps us to meet the needs of people

The effectiveness of your communication skills may depend on how far your approach meets the needs of the other person. For example, you will have to approach a 3-year-old child differently from the way you approach your tutor. Language, posture, pace and tone all need to be adapted to the other person.

Think about yourself for a moment. What needs do you have? In 1954 the psychologist Maslow suggested that people have a hierarchy of needs starting from very basic biological needs, such as food, warmth and going to the toilet, right up to more complex psychological needs. It is only when the basic needs have been met that it is possible to work on fulfilling other needs.

Activity 29

Look at the diagram below and try to think of an example for each stage of need. In what ways might people's age and background affect their needs?

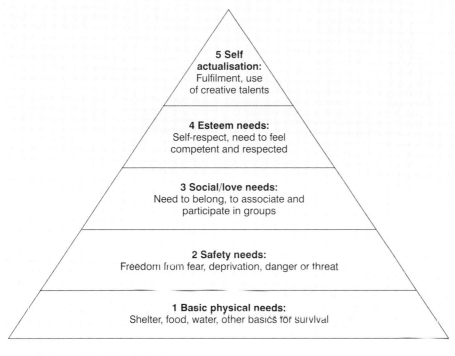

5 Self actualisation:
Fulfilment, use of creative talents

4 Esteem needs:
Self-respect, need to feel competent and respected

3 Social/love needs:
Need to belong, to associate and participate in groups

2 Safety needs:
Freedom from fear, deprivation, danger or threat

1 Basic physical needs:
Shelter, food, water, other basics for survival

Maslow's hierarchy of needs

Non-verbal communication

A large part of communication is actually carried out without speaking – 'non-verbally'. We call this non-verbal communication or body language.

Activity 30

List some of the signs or gestures you know that do not involve speech – without being rude!

Smiling

One of the most significant signs is a smile. Obviously, there are times when it would be inappropriate to smile or grin, if people are upset or very anxious, but in introductions smiling shows warmth and openness, which makes for positive interaction.

You do need to be aware of your own usual facial expression, which can affect the interaction. If you know your group well it may be useful to go round and say how people usually appear. Some people look permanently worried or unhappy – they may not be; but that is the way they come across.

DON'T WORRY, IT MAY NEVER HAPPEN!

Eye contact

This is one of the most direct ways of communicating. Many of you will have received romantic intentions or made them clear without speaking a word!

Certainly, there are many phrases in the English language that illustrate the power of eye contact in communication, such as 'she has shifty eyes', 'he had a gleam in his eye', 'he looked daggers at her'. It may be disconcerting at first to try to communicate deeply with someone who is wearing dark glasses!

Where you focus your eyes makes a difference to the interaction, or two-way talk, you achieve. The length of your gaze also makes a difference. It is not a good idea to stare the client out but it is necessary to look at the client so that they know they have your attention.

People may not be able to return your eye contact for a whole host of reasons. They may be shy, timid, nervous, for example, or unfamiliar with eye contact because they have not been encouraged to look directly

The length of your gaze also makes a difference

at people in their way of life. Some cultures teach that it is impolite to look directly at people, particularly if they are above you socially. If someone has a sight problem then you may think about concentrating on the other senses because they miss out on the eye contact. The tone of your voice becomes more important and you may touch an elbow to gain attention or to reassure them that you are listening. In all these cases you may have to take care that you are not 'put off' by the lack of eye contact. There are other ways of developing rapport (mutual understanding). If you are talking to an individual child, it is sometimes worth saying gently, 'Look at me when I talk to you.'

Posture

Think whether your body language conveys messages like, 'Yes, I am listening. I want to hear what you say', or, 'No, I'm eager to leave. I'm not interested.' Sitting beside the person you are talking to without distractions or 'blocks' like desks separating you makes the difference between good and poor communication patterns. Stretching back in your chair away from the person sends messages of distance and carelessness. Leaning forward, nodding, saying 'yes' or making quiet utterances reinforces your interest to the client.

Think whether your body language conveys messages

Gestures

Hands

How do we use our hands in communication? Drumming fingers implies impatience, as might jangling keys in pockets or twiddling thumbs. Sometimes people use their hands to cover their faces and this may imply that they have something to hide – they are being defensive. It is also difficult sometimes to hear what someone is saying if they cover their face!

If you rub your nose or eyes, this may be interpreted as another barrier or form of avoidance. Scratching your head or neck is often a sign of uncertainty. So if someone says 'I know what you mean' while scratching their head, they may not actually understand at all.

If someone clenches their hands while talking, what might it imply? Wringing the hands conveys anxiety and one wrist gripping the other may indicate frustration or that the person is trying to gain self-control.

Arms and legs

Folding arms implies that a person has something to hide. This is a negative gesture – it puts a barrier between you and the other person. A partial armfold may indicate being unsure or lacking in self-confidence. This may be reinforced if the head is down. If a person holds their head up, on the other hand, they are more sure of themselves. Notice in group situations that if someone disagrees, their head may go down or go from side to side in a 'No, no' gesture.

Like arms, legs can also be positioned in a defensive way, as a barrier. Crossed legs and leaning back from the client may signal avoidance and feelings of superiority. Of course, people may sit with crossed legs because they feel more comfortable that way and not because of any defence mechanism. Crossed legs with a swinging foot, however, may signal flippancy and a tapping foot clearly suggests impatience.

Activity 31

Be aware of other people's body language. Observe how people respond in tense or awkward situations, if they are wearing new clothes, or if they want to impress or attract someone.

If someone has a hearing impairment, non-verbal communication becomes even more significant and special training in signing may be necessary.

When you are with young children it may be necessary to exaggerate non-verbal communication in order to gain or maintain their attention. If you are working in a school, you will find it useful to observe how much non-verbal communication the teacher uses.

It may be necessary to exaggerate non-verbal communication to maintain their attention

People with learning difficulties may use 'makaton', a form of sign language, which gives them some way to communicate.

People with learning difficulties may use Makaton to communicate

Activity 32

In pairs discuss the reasons why it is necessary for everyone to be able to find some way of communicating. Make a note of the reasons and share them with the rest of the group.

Touch

Keep your hands off me!

This is a very tricky aspect of non-verbal communication and needs some confidence. Occasionally a hand on someone's shoulder or arm can be very reassuring, and with children, giving a hug after a bad fall can be a spontaneous response to a distressed child. You can only act according to the client, the situation and your own response.

The issue of physical contact can easily be misunderstood or misrepresented if it is retold in the wrong way. This is particularly true if different genders are involved, for example, in the case of a male nursery nurse working with children. In this sense your actions must always be above any criticism. Other staff must be involved.

Space/distance

Have you ever noticed how people stand a safe distance apart when they don't know each other? Have you ever felt uncomfortable when somebody you don't know has edged on to your side of the seat on a train or on a bus? Some people actually stand very close to you when they talk and it makes you feel uneasy.

Activity 33

In pairs try to have conversations at different distances apart. Work out which one suits you best. Choose easy subjects of conversation such as hobbies, music, pets or television programmes. What is the preferred distance?

Everyone has their own 'personal space'. This is the space that they need for themselves where only those they know well can enter. When people are compelled to be near each other for some reason, in a railway carriage, for example, they often adopt little mechanisms to avoid catching the eye of the other person, such as staring out of the window, or concentrating on the newspaper or a book.

When you are relating to an individual, be careful not to stand or sit too close to them. They may feel that their personal space has been suddenly invaded and 'draw back' from talking. On the other hand, you do need to be able to hear each other!

Barriers to effective communication

You may be bewildered by the many points raised in connection with developing communication skills, but if you hang on to one thing it should be that everyone is unique and needs a unique response.

However much you practise, however far you go in the caring profession, there will be no two people to whom you can respond in exactly the same way. That is why working with people is never boring. It may be that you study some information about a particular culture or religion and then meet someone from that culture. You may feel confident that you know about them but you do not know them. You can only know them by talking to them, relating to them and spending time with them.

So you can work on improving your listening skills, your questioning skills and be conscious of your body language. Other physical or practical factors may inhibit or prevent good interaction with the other person – factors like noise, interruptions from other people or from you, or barriers such as desks or chairs. Sometimes the room temperature may be so cold or so hot that it is difficult to concentrate on the matter in hand. Someone may be very tired or hungry. Children and many others find it hard to take in what is being said if they are tired, thirsty or hungry.

As well as physical barriers affecting your rapport with the other person, there may be language problems or a speech difficulty that slows down the interaction.

There will be many occasions when the other person finds it difficult to talk because of emotional factors such as anger, shame or great sadness. Can you think of other emotional factors that might prevent interaction?

Case study

Mabel Atkin suffers badly with arthritis and has a heart condition. She has lived most of her life in a council house where she brought up her three children, who are now married and have moved away. She found the house too difficult to keep clean and tidy in spite of being extremely houseproud. She had a serious heart attack and much against her will decided she needed care in a residential situation. She watched her house being packed up; there wasn't time for a preliminary visit to the home arranged by her son. Her belongings and furniture were mostly put in a skip as they were too old and tatty for her family. Sadly she had to say goodbye to Jasper, her pet dog. She hates the restriction of the room in the home after being in the big house. She smokes and is very much overweight so the staff are trying to do something about this. She is upset that someone has marked her clothes and underwear with 'Room 13'. She doesn't know one care assistant from another – they keep changing and some of them are only slips of girls telling her what to do. She thinks she should be doing her own washing and cooking.

Write a brief report about how Mrs Atkin might be feeling and what her initial responses to care might be.

Look again at Mrs Atkin and work out what support she needs.

Q How might her admission to the home have been made less traumatic?

Q How might her feelings to the carers be demonstrated?

Q Think of her seeing the manager of the residential home in her own home.

Q How could the situation have been made easier?

Q How could the staff of the home have been briefed?

Q How far are the staff right to try to do something about Mrs Atkin's smoking and eating?

Answers to questions in Activity 17

	Intention	Method	Effect
a	Not racist	Racist	Racist
b	Not racist	Not racist	Racist
c	Not racist	Not racist	Racist

Key terms

After reading this unit you should be able to understand the following words and phrases. If you do not, go back through the unit and find out, or look them up in the Glossary.

Primary Care Group
Purchaser and provider
GP fundholder
NHS Trust
Primary Health Group
Referral
Practice nurse
Communication skills

Verbal communication
Non-verbal communication
Care value base
Non-judgemental attitude
Antidiscriminatory practice
Prejudice
Confidentiality
Code of practice

Test yourself

1 What is meant by the terms 'purchaser and provider'?
2 How many different ways are there for a client to be referred for support?
3 What was the new name given to Family Practitioner Committees under the National Health and Community Care Act 1990?
4 How do the roles of a hospital nurse and a practice nurse differ?
5 What does NHS Direct do?

6 What are the main responsibilities of the Social Services Committee?
7 What are the main responsibilities of a Primary Care Group?
8 What is a health care trust?
9 What kind of people are likely to ask for the services of a health visitor?

Assignment

Produce a service profile based on two different health and/or social care settings, which includes:

the organisation of the services and the roles of people who work in them, how the care value base underpins work in supporting clients, relevant codes of practice or charters and ways in which different types of communication skills are used in care settings.

You have been placed for work experience in a local home for elderly people. The manager has asked you to produce a report that can be given to other students who will be placed in the home. This report must include the following.

To gain a merit or distinction you are asked to *analyse* certain situations or tasks. Analysing means *breaking the task down into detailed parts* – if you are to analyse job roles you must present a lot of detail about the work the person is expected to carry out.

Tasks

1 Correctly identify the care sector and client group for each setting.

2 Thoroughly explore the roles of two workers, correctly identify and explain the care value base that underpins their work.

3 Describe the use of any codes of practice or charters that relate to the organisation in which the workers are based.

4 Show your ability to use relevant communication skills and give accurate explanation of possible barriers to communication with clients.

5 Analyse the job roles that you have chosen and compare the way in which the care value base is implemented in day-to-day work in the two different settings.

6 Explain fully how codes of practice and charters help to protect users of the services.

Get the grade

To get a **PASS** you must complete tasks 1–4

To get a **MERIT** you must complete tasks 1–7

To get a **DISTINCTION** you must complete tasks 1–10

7 Give an explanation of the communication methods you chose to use, identifying your strengths and weaknesses.

8 Show a high level of understanding of the care settings and the work roles of staff in the settings by explaining how work roles are influenced by the sector and type of organisation.

9 Show realistic proposals for improving your communication skills.

10 Give an evaluation of the effectiveness of codes of practice and charters in upholding the care value base.

Key Skills   Opportunity

	You can use this Assignment to provide evidence for the following Key Skills
Communication C2.1a	1 When interviewing workers about their jobs 2 When demonstrating your communication skills
Communication C2.1b	When you orally present your report
Communication C2.2	Investigating the different care/health settings
Communication C2.3	Reporting on the different care settings

Promoting health and well-being

What is covered in this unit

At the end of this unit you will be asked to produce a plan for promoting health and well-being for at least one person who is at risk. If you would like to see further details of the tasks you are likely to need to carry out for assessment please refer to the end of the unit where an assignment has been set (see pp. 157–8). This unit will guide you through what you need to know in order to successfully put together the plan. You will be assessed on this work and awarded a grade. This grade will contribute to the overall grade you will get for Unit Two.

Materials you will need to complete this unit

- *The Balance of Good Health*, Department of Health and the Ministry of Agriculture, Fisheries and Food
- *Manual of Nutrition*, Ministry of Agriculture, Fisheries and Food, 1995
- *The Health of the Nation – Low Income and Nutrition and Health (Strategies for Improvement)*, Department of Health, 1996
- Publications from
  - local health education authorities
  - Drug Advisory Service

2.1 What is meant by health and well-being

Everyone wants to be healthy. Sometimes we take being healthy for granted until for some reason we become ill or find it difficult to cope.

In the last decade there has been unprecedented interest on the part of individuals in their own fitness as distinct from health care. Many people, however, want to participate in their own health care and governments are keen to encourage them, in order to cut down on increasing health costs. In 1978 the World Health Organization's Declaration of Alma Ata stated that it was the right and duty of people to participate collectively and as individuals in their own health care.

'Health' comes from an Old English word meaning 'whole'. Health encompasses physical, emotional, intellectual and social well-being. **Health and well-being** should mean that a person feels positively well and is not just free of disease or illness. It is difficult to define and collect information about 'well-being' as it often relates to how individual people feel about themselves and their personal experiences. 'Well-being' is therefore more difficult to define than illness as it is often taken for granted. People do not usually go about saying they are 'well'. Well-being could be described as the attainment of an individual's potential.

What are the four basic needs of individuals?

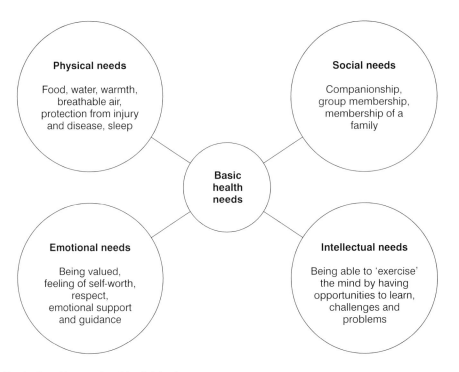

Basic health needs of individuals

Basic needs do not change. The differences are in the ability of an individual to provide for his or her own needs. Put another way, people need different amounts and types of support to meet their needs throughout life.

Different needs also have differing importance:

1   The need for food and shelter and water means that they are essential to stay alive.
2   The next important need is for safety.
3   Having achieved the first two, a person is in need of emotional and social support.
4   Only when all these needs have been met is it realistic to consider needs for self-respect and **self-esteem** and, finally, personal fulfilment.

For example, people who are starving may take risks that could affect their health and well-being or degrade themselves by doing things they would not do if they were fully fed. Their primary need is for food and only later can they consider their self-respect. This 'hierarchy of needs' was described by a researcher called Abraham Maslow (see Unit One page 63).

Information and choice

Information is the first step towards making healthy choices. Consider how healthy you are. You know how unpleasant it is to feel unwell, but what does being healthy really mean? A person who is in good health is someone whose body is working at maximum efficiency, mentally and physically.

Here are some factors that affect your health:

- genetic inheritance
- age
- gender
- environment
- organisms, microbes, parasites
- education
- national services relating to health and welfare
- climate
- pollution
- social class.

List four factors that could affect your health.

In addition to these factors, increasing attention is being paid to 'lifestyle' factors. Why do cancer, heart disease and strokes occur particularly in our western society? The quest to find out is known as epidemiology. Epidemiologists are now identifying 'lifestyle' factors, particularly diet and lack of exercise, as causes of health problems. We all have the power to influence our own health and that of our family.

Activity 1

a Write down what you do in a typical week in terms of:
  i rest
  ii relaxation
  iii sleep
  iv exercise
  v recreation
  vi work and/or study.

Give approximate daily timings for each activity and the total amount.

b What sort of pattern is there to your week? Is there a balance of different types of activity?

Compare and discuss your notes with other members of your group.

Community health and hygiene

Nowadays we expect:

- good-quality housing
- clean cities and towns
- good town planning
- unspoiled country and coastal areas
- clean, wholesome water
- clean milk
- clean air
- clean, safe food
- effective sewage disposal
- high levels of vaccination to prevent outbreaks of infectious diseases
- effective refuse disposal.

Activity 2

Divide into small groups. Each group should study one or more services relating to public health and hygiene, such as water, sewage or housing.

In your town or area:

a Find out all you can about the services. Collect leaflets and information.
b Note how the service is provided, for example, by the local authority, a private company or contracted out to a private organisation.
c Find out what the costs of the service are to individuals.
d Present your findings to the rest of your group. Keep a note in your file of your contribution to this work.

Factors affecting health and well-being

Problem	Possible effects
Poor housing Old – in need of modernisation Inappropriate for user group Overcrowded Lacking in adequate sanitary facilities Damp	Stress Increased accident rate Infections Respiratory problems
Poor-quality water Dirty – untreated Contaminated with micro-organisms Excess levels of chemicals, e.g. nitrates	Gastric upsets Dysentery Hepatitis Typhoid Cholera
Inadequate sewage facilities Poor drainage treatment Old drains that need replacing Untreated sewage getting into water supply Untreated sewage in areas where people bathe	Water-borne infections, such as gastro-enteritis, dysentery, hepatitis, typhoid, polio, cholera
Inadequate refuse disposal arrangements Poor facilities for collecting rubbish Lack of proper refuse disposal sites	Infestations of: • rats and mice, causing food poisoning (and possibly Weil's disease, a rare jaundice spread in rats' urine) • flies, causing gastro-enteritis, dysentery, typhoid, cholera

2.2 Aspects of health and well-being that differ between different people and groups

The nutritional needs of different people

To ensure adequate **nutrition**, people have different dietary needs at different times in their lives.

Young children

Young children have a great need for protein, thiamin and calcium as they grow, particularly at around 7–8 years of age. Some children may find it difficult to eat well for a variety of reasons.

Activity 3

Make a list of things that might affect a child's eating pattern.

Adolescents

Adolescents also have high nutritional needs. They may find it difficult to eat balanced meals because they are busy or because they may not care for food prepared by their parents and considered to be nourishing. They may miss meals because of demands on their time.

This is also a time when they may be aware of their body shape and feel they need to lose or gain weight. Adolescence is a vulnerable time for eating disorders such as anorexia and bulimia. Sometimes young people are influenced by media images of what they should eat, what they should drink and how they should appear. Emotionally, adolescence can be a turbulent time and eating can be seen as an escape or a comfort at a time of possible exam pressure, career dilemma, parental tension and relationship worries. Apart from all that, some people do enjoy their adolescent years!

Adults

Adults may be concerned about time and costs in connection with food. This is particularly the case if they work and have family responsibilities and/or if they are on a low income.

Sometimes people fail to eat well because they are anxious or stressed about matters that are important to them, such as relationships, family and work or lack of work. The reverse situation can also happen, when people overeat possibly because they feel it doesn't matter about weight as they grow older or possibly because they are overwrought or overworked. There are many reasons why people overeat or become overweight. You might like to discuss some of these reasons in class. Think about decreased mobility and the calorie levels of alcoholic drinks.

Pregnant women and breast-feeding mothers

This group of women need high quantities of protein, iron, calcium, folic acid (a B-group vitamin) and vitamins C and D. Sometimes the minerals and vitamins are prescribed by the GP, but a good nutritional intake is also required.

Elderly people

Elderly people may have fewer energy requirements because of decreased mobility and a smaller appetite. There are also social reasons why elderly people may not eat well. They may live alone and it may seem pointless to cook for one.

They may be on a fixed income and find it difficult to afford the food they would like to eat. They may find it hard to shop and many pre-packed goods may be too much for them.

They may find it physically difficult to cook.

They may get little or no pleasure from eating because of false teeth, diminished sense of smell, etc.

Activity 4

What might you suggest to improve nutrition in each of the cases listed above? What can be done to improve nutrition?

People with a disability

People with a disability are no more likely to be nutritionally deficient than any other group. It depends on the nature of the disability and the individual concerned. Where mobility is restricted, weight gain may be a problem, in which case a reduced calorie intake may be necessary. If you need to plan or cook meals for children or people with disabilities, then you will need to check their dietary requirements with them or with their carers.

Diabetics

Diabetics have a metabolic disorder (diabetes) that reduces the body's ability to control the amount of glucose in the blood. Diabetics need to avoid the rapid rises in blood glucose that result from eating large amounts of readily absorbed **carbohydrate**. Their total carbohydrate intake needs to be controlled. Asian diabetics tend to live well, eating rice or chapatis, which means that 60% of their diet is carbohydrate (coming from rice and chapatis); on the other hand, traditional low carbohydrate diets may be high in fat, which can lead to heart disease.

Planning meals

What's for tea? What would you like for your supper? When did you last eat a proper meal?

Many factors influence what we eat: habit, age, class, income, available money, taste, family background, amount of time we have, who we are with, whether we play sport, etc.

A balanced meal is said to be one with adequate amounts of carbohydrate, protein, minerals, **vitamins** and fibre, but low in sugar, fat and salt.

There is no point in knowing about **nutrients** if we do not put that knowledge into practice. Before you plan to eat you should consider these questions:

- What pattern of eating suits my way of living?
- What foods are available and what can I afford?
- Is there anyone in my family who has special dietary needs?
- How do I ensure that I obtain the necessary nutrients?

The nutrient triangle

Most of us prepare meals without really thinking about their nutritional value. We think more about the likes and dislikes of the people who will be eating the meal. While we want to avoid food being wasted, it is important to include foods in each meal that satisfy our dietary needs. No matter what race or culture we belong to, it is possible to provide meals that are healthy and satisfy the family's likes and dislikes.

If you divide the main nutrients into three groups then the triangle that they form can be used to check whether the meal you are planning is balanced or not.

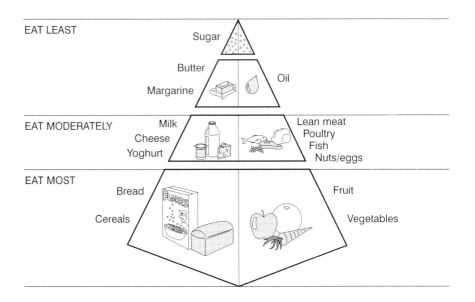

The nutrient triangle

Remember that too many energy foods can cause obesity and that fruit and vegetables should be used to supply the bulk of fibre in our diet.

quick fire

Which group has the higher nutritional needs – children or less active people?

Energy requirements

Different people need different amounts of food each day. The amount needed depends on age, sex, size and activity level. People with high energy needs, such as children, manual workers and teenagers, will need more energy than less active people. Sedentary people (people who do not take much exercise) may need to cut down on energy foods.

Activity 5

a Plan two days' meals for yourself and a friend. How have you ensured that you are getting the right amounts of nutrients?

b Plan two days' meals for someone with particular dietary needs. (He or she could be elderly/vegetarian/of a different cultural background.) How have you ensured that his or her dietary needs are being met?

Activity 6

Look at the drawings in the picture below.

The benefits of regular exercise

Check whether anyone in your group can verify one or more of the points on the previous page. Ask them how they feel about exercise.

*a simple guide to **ACTIVE** living for adults*

Exercise

For some people, the mere mention of the word 'exercise' makes them shrink away. This reaction may be the result of unhappy experiences of exercise and, particularly, of competitive sport. In the early 1990s the Sports Council carried out a survey of people's fitness levels and the activities they carried out. The results were disturbing: one in three men and two in three women were unable to walk at a reasonable pace up a slope without becoming breathless. This happens because most people do not take adequate regular exercise. Exercise is an extremely individual matter. People can select from a whole range of exercise patterns and sports to find something which suits their level and their lifestyle.

What are the benefits of exercise?

If you try, you will enjoy exercise. You will also feel better for it – eventually! Even if you have exercised regularly, it is easy to lose the habit if you give up for a short time, particularly if you have just embarked on a new course and changed your social environment.

Regular exercise improves:

- stamina
- suppleness
- strength.

The table below illustrates the benefits from various physical activities. Bear in mind, however, that the actual benefits will depend on how vigorously the activity is carried out.

The benefits of various physical activities

Activity	Stamina rating	Suppleness rating	Strength rating
Badminton	2	3	2
Canoeing	3	2	3
Climbing stairs	3	1	2
Cricket	1	2	1
Cycling (hard)	4	2	3
Dancing (ballroom)	1	3	1
Dancing (disco)	3	4	1
Football	3	3	3
Golf	1	2	1
Gymnastics	2	4	3
Hillwalking	3	1	2
Jogging	4	2	2
Judo	2	4	2
Rowing	4	2	4
Sailing	1	2	2
Swimming (hard)	4	4	4
Tennis	2	3	2
Walking (briskly)	2	1	1
Weightlifting	1	1	4
Yoga	1	4	1

Key: 1 = no real effect   2 = beneficial effect
       3 = very good effect   4 = excellent effect

List two benefits of exercise.

Regular exercise

If you exercise vigorously but spasmodically, you are shocking your body into action and your muscles are jolted into performance. On the other hand, if you exercise gradually at first and then build up regularly, your body becomes accustomed to the pressure. Limbs become more flexible and your heart and lungs increase their capacity to supply the body with its extra demands for oxygen.

People are less likely to maintain an exercise plan if it is not suited to their lifestyle.

It is far better to set them realistic targets that you know they can fit into their routine – such as running a couple of miles before tea or before dark, twice a week – than proposing a time-consuming or expensive sport. It is better for their self-esteem to keep to a regular exercise pattern than to start and then trail off.

Exercise routines

Exercise routines can be divided into two types:

What does aerobic exercise do to the body?

Aerobic – exercise that works the heart, lungs and blood system, such as running, fast swimming and fast cycling.

83

- **Anaerobic** – exercise that concentrates on stretching and flexing the muscles, such as yoga and general stretch work.

A good exercise programme will combine the two types of exercise, depending on individual needs.

Whichever activity you choose with people, encourage them to build up gradually. To gain and maintain a fitness level they ought to aim for three 20-minute sessions per week. Exercise that is boring, gruelling or difficult to fit in with their lifestyle will be a problem to maintain. Choose something they feel happy with and that is not too disruptive of their routine at work and home. You may encourage their friends and family to join them.

Another point concerning anaerobic work is that some people of average flexibility try to work at levels that are beyond them and injury results.

People should try to:

- warm up thoroughly
- avoid jerky movements
- avoid exercises that leave the back unsupported like the 'bridge' ((a) in the illustration below)
- take care doing double-leg raises (b) or exercises that involve lifting the leg high to a fixed point (c)
- be cautious doing sit-ups with straight legs (d).

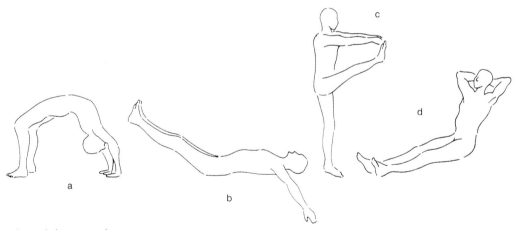

Take care when doing exercises

Questions people should consider before exercise

- Can they afford the cost of the exercise?
- Are they fit or do they need a medical check-up?
- Do they have suitable clothes?
- Do they have suitable footwear?
- Is the weather suitable and safe for the exercise?
- Do they have enough time to warm up before and cool down after?
- Have they eaten enough and sufficiently early so that the food is digested?

Monitoring exercise

You will find it encouraging to monitor the person's progress in terms of how fit they are getting during the training programme.

Pulse rate

Taking a person's pulse is one way of monitoring their fitness. The slower their pulse the fitter they are getting.

To check a pulse, press the artery on the inside of the person's wrist with your first three fingers. Count how many beats you can feel in 10 seconds and then multiply by six; alternatively, count the number of beats you can feel in 60 seconds. The average **pulse rate** is about 70 beats per minute but it may vary according to client group.

Now that you can check their pulse try a few exercises to monitor their fitness level:

List one way to monitor a person's fitness.

- Ask them to walk up and down a flight of steps, say 15–20 in total. On the whole, if they are more than mildly breathless and their pulse is higher than average then they may be unfit. Get them to run on the spot for about 3 minutes. If their pulse is over 90 and they are mildly breathless then they are fairly unfit.
- Using a firm bench or the second step of a stair, ask them to step up and down briskly, for about two steps up and down every 6 seconds for about 3 minutes. If they are very breathless and their pulse rate is about 90 then they are pretty unfit.
- Ask them to jog gently for about one mile. This should take about 10 minutes. If they are not breathless then they are fairly fit.

Recreation and health and well-being

Taking part in recreational activities can reduce **stress** and also improve your physical health. After work or studying, a complete change is good for you. Do you know what is available in your locality?

Leisure or recreational activities include physical pursuits such as sport and walking and less physical activities such as watching sport or TV, meeting friends, reading and listening to music. Leisure or recreational activities can mean different things to different people, depending on their situation and interests. Some people may like DIY, others may like walking or reading. Leisure activities of all sorts contribute to health and well-being and to the quality of people's lives.

Surveys carried out in the United Kingdom indicate that indoor leisure pursuits are more common than outdoor ones. Watching TV is the most popular activity; going out for a drink is an activity enjoyed by over half of people interviewed. What factors influence people's ability to take part in recreational activities? Social or cultural values may influence women's ability to take part in sport. If people enjoyed activities as children then they are more likely to take part in them as adults. Participation may also be restricted because of cost, lack of time or access difficulties. People on low incomes may not be able to afford the cost of

What is the most popular recreational activity?

entrance fees and people with disabilities may not be able to take part because of inadequate physical access.

Activity 7

a Make a list of all the recreational activities in which you participate.

b List any things that would restrict your access to these activities.

c Find out about recreational activities in your local area. Produce a concise booklet which would inform teenagers about activities that are available.

Recreational activities

What you do as a break from work is important to your health and well-being. Recreational activities can be classified as those involving:

- physical exercise (see above)
- other people in a social setting
- intellectual activity.

Some activities may fall into more than one of these groups. For example:

- Dancing is a physical activity in a social setting.
- A quiz night is an intellectual activity in a social setting.

The activities are all linked because they involve the development and maintenance of physical, social, emotional and intellectual well-being.

Recreation can overlap different classes of activity. Dancing involves exercise as well as being a social activity

Physical benefits of recreation

Physical activity contributes to fitness in several ways:

- strength – the ability of muscles to work over short periods of time. It is required for lifting or in the act of jumping.
- stamina – the ability for muscles to continue working without fatigue (becoming tired).
- suppleness – the flexibility of the joints. Exercise to develop suppleness is part of warming up and avoids strains to muscles and joints.
- speed of reaction – the ability to respond rapidly to changes. This is linked to things like hand–eye co-ordination. Linked to these are improved balance and agility.
- heart and lung efficiency (how well they work) – regular physical recreation makes the heart, lungs and circulation work. The exercise improves their abilities to provide oxygen to the body. This has the benefit of reducing risks of heart disease.
- determination – regular physical activity has a knock-on effect in providing the determination to follow tasks through to a finish.

List three physical benefits of physical activity.

Different physical activities develop different aspects of fitness. Jogging and dancing develop stamina. Gymnastics improves suppleness. Badminton improves strength, suppleness and stamina.

Clearly, activities need to be balanced with ability and age. Well thought-out physical recreation provides benefits to physical health. It is also important to recognise that there are many activities that are not considered to be sports but that also contribute to physical health, such as recreational dancing and walking for pleasure.

Problem-solving provides mental stimulation for people of all ages

Intellectual benefits

You may think that all your mental activity should be confined to school or college. Recreation should be relaxing. Intellectual activity can, however, provide a stimulating, satisfying and, at the same time, relaxing recreation. This type of activity often involves problem-solving in some way. This may be in terms of strategy, in games like chess.

Reading also provides an intellectual stimulus. Reading for relaxation can involve stories that stimulate your imagination. Using your imagination stimulates mental activity and satisfaction in the enjoyment of the story. Many books also involve problem-solving as part of the enjoyment. Mysteries and detective stories often give sufficient information to enable you to solve the problem before the main characters do.

Problem-solving activities and using your imagination both lead to a more active mind. You can use your experiences from reading to help make connections and solve problems for yourself in your life. Strategy games or books that involve thinking about choices help to make you analyse questions, such as 'What would happen if . . .?' This can carry over into your daily activities, where you start to think further about the consequences of your actions.

Many hobbies that involve collecting, learning new skills (such as playing musical instruments) or making objects (models or pottery) involve intellectual skills. Meeting with others with similar likes in clubs and societies provides some of the social benefits of recreation.

List two recreational activities that would give intellectual stimulus.

Social and emotional benefits

People are not naturally social animals: they have to learn how to be sociable. One of the worst possible tortures is to deprive a person of contact with other people. To be social animals we need to know how to interact with other people.

Young children often appear to be very selfish. They do not know how to share. They always want things for themselves and their needs are most important. Many recreational activities for young children help them to learn about playing with other children and sharing. A major importance of pre-school activities is in learning these social skills. A second important aspect is to see many different children acting in different ways. These different role models help the child to learn how to interact with other people.

The need for social contact is recognised in most caring systems. For older people, there is a risk of isolation. Where a husband or wife dies the surviving partner may be left to live alone in a house with little contact with other people. This isolation can be worsened by difficulties in moving out of the house. Many Social Services departments recognise this and organise day centres to support people by bringing them together for social interaction. Other recreational activities are often provided to support this.

Dances, bingo and special swimming sessions for pensioners, for example, can all be provided to help maintain social interaction.

Any social interaction helps people to understand each other. For adolescents, the social interaction may be in situations where individuals can start to explore relationships. Youth clubs, discos and youth organisations provide an opportunity for individuals to meet and learn about each other. In some cases, these relationships may develop further into friendship or, in some cases, marriage.

Shared recreational activities imply shared interests. This is the first step towards friendship. The benefits of recreational activities are normally a mixture of physical, intellectual and social. The mixture contributes to a balanced personality and a balanced lifestyle.

Activity 8

Read the comments below. Describe the benefits each young person is gaining from his or her activities.

a 'I really enjoy playing tennis. Even though sometimes I feel a bit lethargic, I know when I start to warm up that I'll feel better. I seem to have more energy when I play than when I don't bother going down to the sessions.'

b 'When I've been working in the evening, I look forward to going to the coffee bar. It gives me a chance to catch up on the gossip, to relax and unwind with my friends.'

c 'I like the challenge of climbing, of pushing myself to the limit of taking a risk. Although I'm scared, it's still a thrilling experience.'

d 'I need to get out of the house a bit at weekends. That's why I like to meet up with my friends and go to a club. I need to talk to people of my own age. I notice when I've been away from home on outdoor pursuits weeks with the Duke of Edinburgh's Award team, I appreciate home more. I think I need to have my own space – some independence.'

e 'I like going away on training weekends with St John's. It's interesting thinking about meeting new people and even more interesting when you might arrange to see someone again afterwards.'

f 'I'm not much good at art really, but I love painting, using colour. I feel really free when I settle down to paint, focused but free – strange, really.'

g 'I often spend time writing. Sometimes it helps to order my thoughts, sometimes it's just good to imagine situations and let the pen run. I like being by myself for a while too.'

▶▶

h 'We have some really good discussions down at the youth group. The sessions really make me think about big issues like politics, religion and relationships.'

i 'When I'm at school, I feel I'm one of a huge number, but when I'm helping with the play scheme, I feel important, wanted and useful.'

How did you get on? Could you describe how the activities were of value to the young people? Did you think about how they might need physical challenges, company of people their own age, time to relax, chances to take risks, time to be away from parents, opportunities to meet people, chances to make friends with the opposite gender, time to be alone, space to concentrate, an opportunity to sort out what they really think, a way of raising self-esteem and self-identity?

Benefits of recreation for different people

From Activity 8, you will have the tools to help you to consider aspects of recreational activities that affect choice. Broadly speaking, the different groups of people to consider are:

- children
- adolescents
- elderly people
- families.

For activities to be beneficial they need to match the needs and abilities of the individuals. There should also be a balance in terms of physical, social and intellectual pursuits.

Children

Most of us would consider the major recreational activity for children to be play. Play provides physical, intellectual and social benefits. The type of play will depend upon the stage of development that the child is at. Some physical activities, such as swimming, are appropriate for all ages of child. Other activities, such as team games (football, hockey, netball, etc.), require physical, intellectual and social development before they are appropriate. Young children may not have:

- the physical co-ordination to catch or hit a ball
- the intellectual development to understand rules
- the social development to play co-operatively in a team.

What recreational activities are suitable for children?

Young children

For young children, much of their recreation occurs in and around the home. Often it involves supervision and co-operation by an adult. Typical activities and the areas that they address might include:

- drawing, painting and colouring – physical and intellectual
- looking at books – intellectual
- playing with dolls – social, emotional and intellectual
- dressing up – intellectual, emotional and social
- pretend cooking – intellectual, emotional, social and physical.

The list could, of course, be extended. Most toys for young children support their need for physical, social and intellectual activities.

For most children, recreation involving social interaction with other children takes place with friends in the home or in organised groups. Organised groups include playgroups, creches and nurseries. These groups also provide recreational activities that clearly support physical and intellectual needs.

Some organised physical recreational activities are available for young children. Most swimming pools have specific times for parents and young children. Gymnastic activities are also available in association with national gymnastic associations. Both of these clearly provide for physical recreation.

Many local authorities provide playgrounds for children, with climbing frames, swings and slides. These offer opportunities for recreation, particularly physical but also involving social interaction. Fantasy play, for example by turning the climbing frame into a fortress, is a form of intellectual recreation.

Activity 9

This activity can take place anywhere that children play. It is important that any adults present know what you are doing. It would be a suitable activity for a work placement.

Observe a young child playing. List the different activities being undertaken in a period of 15 minutes.

Next to each activity write down the areas it benefits (physical, intellectual or social).

Examples of young children undertaking social and intellectual recreation

Older children

As children get older the availability of organised recreational activities increases. The child's development makes organised team games possible. Parental involvement may become less and the child may undertake some recreation away from home and parental supervision. Growing independence can make playgrounds and parks more available.

There are many organisations that provide supported recreation for children. They include national provision through organisations like the Scouts, Guides and Woodcraft Folk. Each of these supports recreational activities across a wide age range.

Physical recreation through team sports, swimming and gymnastics are frequently organised by schools, sports or leisure centres. Such centres also organise discos for children, providing both social and physical recreation.

Normally, as children get older they learn to read. Reading becomes available as a form of recreation. It also makes games with written rules available for recreational activities.

Childhood is also a time when hobbies develop. Often these involve:

- model-making in some form
- collecting
- developing skills in dance or playing a musical instrument.

All of these provide an intellectual side to recreation. They also offer opportunities to meet people with similar interests, so bringing in social aspects.

Organisations like the Scouts and the Guides provide opportunities for social, intellectual and physical recreation that might not otherwise be available

Adolescents

This follows on from the developments in childhood. Again, as people get older, their independence increases. Recreation outside the home may be more easy to access. The range of activities includes social gatherings in youth clubs and other organised functions.

For many people this is a time of peak physical fitness. It is also a time when recreation patterns become established and are maintained throughout the rest of life. Access to and availability of recreation facilities can be very important.

The social aspect of recreational activities now becomes very important. It is a time where relationships are being explored and many recreational activities involve social groupings.

Adolescence is a time when gangs or peer groups may form. The term 'gang' sometimes, but not always, describes a group of people who behave in ways that are unacceptable to other people. A gang may form partly because there are no other facilities available for recreational activities.

Social and physical recreation are important aspects of being at a disco

Elders

A common stereotype of elders implies that physical recreation has to be limited. This view is incorrect. What must be taken into account is the need to ensure that the physical recreation is appropriate. Care needs to be taken to ensure that the activities help maintain the body rather than damaging it. Activities can be physically demanding without causing damage.

Elders are not at a peak of physical fitness:

- Reaction speeds reduce with age.
- Bones become more fragile and injuries take longer to heal.
- Heart, lungs and circulation are less efficient in elders.

All of these will affect the choice of activity. Often recreation that is physical and also has a social focus is appropriate.

The stereotypical game for older people is often considered to be bowls. However, it meets the needs on many counts. It involves some physical activity. There is a very strong social element of meeting with other people and having time to talk. The skill of controlling the ball and playing to win involves an intellectual challenge.

Reading is a shared recreation that provides intellectual stimulation. Parents can communicate an enthusiasm for reading to their children

Recreational activities for people with specific needs

So far we have considered recreational activities in general. There are many people who, for a variety of reasons, may have specific recreational needs. For example:

- People living alone need to be able to take part in social activities.
- People with disabilities may need support to take part in some forms of recreation.
- Elderly people may have a variety of specific needs for recreation that reflect age, mobility or living alone.
- Other people may have needs because of their concerns about their own obesity (overweight).

In all of these cases, the choice of recreation has to be made to provide for the need. To suggest that a person living alone undertakes solitary recreation, such as jogging, does not meet the need for social recreation. To encourage an obese person to take up physical activities involving strenuous exercise would be dangerous to his or her health. You would also need to consider the feelings of an obese person, who may be embarrassed to exercise where others might laugh at them.

Many of the issues associated with specific needs can be addressed by increasing awareness of the issues. Let us consider specific groups in more detail.

Activity 10

Read the comments below. Decide what needs are being satisfied by each activity.

a 'When I practise yoga, I feel so completely relaxed that I sleep better and seem to be less harassed during the day.' *Mother of three young children*

b 'I was delighted when Phil was asked to swim for the school. He had been a bit low after that bullying incident.' *Father of a 10-year-old boy*

c 'Sometimes I think I won't go to the day centre when I feel in one of those "can't be bothered" moods. But then I urge myself to get going, have a wash and shave, change my shirt and make an effort. I always feel better for having made the effort. I need that motivation for a bit of self-discipline.' *76-year-old man*

d 'I'm so glad I've mastered the Eureka computer. It gives me chance to write my poems.' *Adolescent girl with very little sight*

e 'I look forward to playing a bit of snooker on Friday nights at the club. I can meet my friends and I'm improving – we have a laugh.' *Teenage boy*

f 'One thing about gardening, it's a good excuse to get out in the fresh air. It's an interest. I look forward to the spring, and in the winter I'm busy with seeds. All that bending and stretching, I don't need to go to keep fit. It's a pity I'm not so enthusiastic about housework!' *Older woman*

g 'I've always danced – I think I danced before I walked! I love to move and I feel I can interpret the music when I dance. The classes help me to improve.' *17-year-old boy*

h 'I can express myself through sculpture. I would like to spend a lot more time on sculpture – working myself and seeing others work.' *Young woman in her early 20s*

i 'Sometimes the reminiscence [when people remember things and discuss them] sessions go really well. You can see the joy in the faces of some of the people when they are reminded of particular things. You can see them grow in self-worth as they link with their past and remember how they once were. I feel I learn a lot too – about them – I appreciate how their lives have changed and I find it easier to relate to them then.' *Occupational therapist in a nursing home*

j 'The simple games and armchair fitness exercises have really improved Mrs Brown's range of movement. She seems brighter in herself now.' *Physiotherapist in a day centre*

k 'You can tell how restless the children become when they miss PE. Last week I took them out on to the field to play some games to release some energy and then we practised some ball skills.' *Infant school teacher*

l 'I enjoyed that quiz we did the other night on old Sheffield. I was really surprised how much they knew. It was fun checking out the answers beforehand. They seemed to chat on for ages afterwards.' *Care assistant in an elderly persons' home*

People with physical disabilities

This covers a wide range of disabilities and may include people who:

- are visually impaired
- are hearing impaired
- are in wheelchairs
- have a limited range of movements (such as severe arthritis)
- have poor muscle control (such as cerebral palsy, Parkinson's disease, multiple sclerosis).

All of these people have one thing in common – they suffer from the attitudes of others. Many well-meaning people try to take control of their lives and tell them what they ought to do in terms of recreation.

While some people with disabilities may feel unable to participate in some recreational activities, most will be able to identify activities that they would like to undertake. In many cases, the recreational activity can be developed to support the specific need.

People with disabilities have the same needs for recreation as everyone else:

- physical recreation
- intellectual recreation.

Physical activities may have an important health-related role in improving mobility, but that is also true for everyone else.

One aspect of physical disability that creates issues for able-bodied people is social recreation. There is a tendency for activities to be organised for people with similar disabilities. These can be very useful as self-help groups, but they do tend to limit contact with others. The reactions of able-bodied people to those with disabilities provides a barrier to many activities in general. This can cause feelings of isolation from society with social links only developing with other people with similar disabilities.

Recreational activities for people with disabilities should cover all of those available in general. Allowances may need to be made for disability. After all, if marathon races were not segregated then few of the runners would have any contact with the competitors in wheelchairs.

It may be necessary to allocate facilities and times specifically for people with disabilities. This goes against much that we have said, but in competitive activities where the disability is significant then it would be reasonable. Other situations should encourage participation of all. Adaptations to the environment are more important than providing separate activities.

SPORT FOR PEOPLE WITH DISABILITIES

THURSDAY LEISURE CLUB
Funtown Leisure Centre
Swimming • Board games • Art Activities
Table tennis • Social activities
7.00–10.00pm
Admission £2
Transport £2

TUESDAY SPORTS CLUB
Anytown Road Sports Centre
Table tennis • Racket games • Cricket
Swimming • Trampolining
6.30–9.30pm
Admission £2
Transport £2

SATURDAY JUNIOR CLUB
Uptown Sports Centre
Short tennis • Football • Badminton
Music club • Swimming • Art Activities
10am–12 noon
Admission £1
Transport £2

SATURDAY CLUB
Uptown Road Sports Centre
Archery • Shooting • Indoor bowls
2–4pm
Admission £3
Transport £2

For further information on all these clubs contact Rob at Uptown Sports Centre. Tel 123456.
Ask for further information on OUTDOOR PURSUITS for people with disabilities

Many recreational facilities are made available to people who find access difficult

People with specific health-related problems

In this category would be obese people and those with heart and circulation problems. There are two issues involved in selecting recreational activities. These are related to:

- self-esteem
- health and safety.

Self-esteem
Any recreational activity that exposes a person to embarrassment will lower his or her self-esteem. An obese person may feel unable to participate in an activity because of the possible comments of others. This is a case where self-help groups can be important.

In health terms, an obese person needs to lose weight. Recreation may be directed to this with physical activity and diet contributing. If the physical activity is carried out with others who are obese, the embarrassment factor can be reduced. There is also an element of understanding and pressure from colleagues, which helps a person to continue in the activity. This social aspect of the recreation is important.

Health and safety
An obese person should undertake physical activity under guidance from a health practitioner. The strain of exercise on joints, muscles and the heart need to be monitored carefully.

General advice is to work up gradually to a high level of physical activity. This enables the body to develop the strength necessary and also encourages weight loss. For this purpose, there are many groups that offer recreation (associated with weight loss) for obese people. For many of these, there is also a cost in money terms that needs to be considered.

Health and safety is also a consideration for people with heart and circulatory problems. Physical recreation needs to be supervised and monitored.

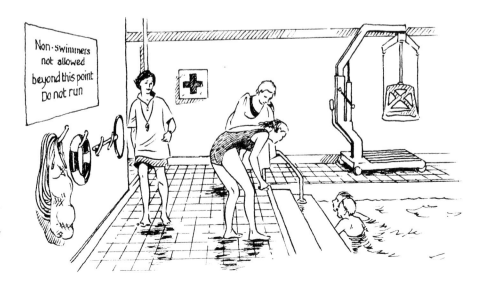

Providers of facilities are concerned about health and safety. Notices and lifeguards remind people of hazards

Swimming is a very appropriate activity for both obese people and those with heart and circulatory disorders. The buoyancy provided by the water reduces the stresses on joints and the exercise can be tailored to meet needs. Swimming provides exercise that improves muscle tone and joint flexibility. It improves breathing and increases the heart rate. Both benefit the respiratory and circulatory systems.

Recreation for elders

Many elders maintain a healthy independent lifestyle. They organise their lives to meet their recreational needs. It is not this group that we will consider.

For some elders, specific recreational support is needed. Those living alone may need support in maintaining social activities. Others may have very little mobility and need assistance in physical activity. There are also needs to provide intellectual stimulation.

Facilities available that provide recreation specifically for elders include day centres and residential homes. Some leisure centres also run specific sessions to support the recreation needs of elders.

A day centre provides a place for social and intellectual recreation for elderly people

Day centres and residential homes provide a variety of activities:

- They provide a place where people meet socially. They offer opportunities for conversation and other forms of social recreation.
- They provide intellectual recreation in a variety of ways.
  - It may be associated with playing games. These may be group games, such as bingo, or individual challenges, such as chess and draughts.

99

  – With some people the intellectual stimulation has to be organised on a one-to-one basis by the care workers. Conversation with care workers involving talking about things that have happened in the past is important. Using photographs and things from the past to stimulate memories also enables people to think about the present.
  – Intellectual recreation can also include activities related to occupational therapy. Intellectual activity may come from concentrating on painting, sewing or knitting. It may come from practising a skill like cooking. All of these also have benefits in physical activity. They do not provide exercise like swimming, but they support fine movements and help maintain hand and finger mobility.

Housing

For many people, home is not only a place of accommodation, but also a source of their physical and mental well-being. Home should be a place where you can relax away from the tensions and pressures of the workplace. A person's house is regarded as their territory. People talk of 'homesickness' when they miss being at home.

People may be judged because of where they live, the type of house they live in and whether it is owned or rented. So housing is much more than bricks and mortar.

How can housing affect personal development and well-being?

During the Second World War, when many thousands of homes were damaged or destroyed, local authorities took the opportunity to clear away the slums and build new homes. In many instances, they replaced this poor housing with high-rise blocks of flats. The flats were generally of a higher standard than the housing they replaced. For the first time people had good sanitation, bathrooms and hot and cold water.

However, rehousing and slum clearances also meant destroying whole neighbourhoods and the feeling of community that existed in them. People who were moved often felt isolated, lonely and missed the support of the extended family – their brothers, sisters, grandparents or aunts or uncles.

The problems associated with high-rise flats caused, in many occupants, mental and emotional stress. Lack of social facilities caused frustration, which in a number of areas led to violence and vandalism. Many local authorities later realised that high-rise flats were a mistake. In recent years, therefore, authorities such as Sheffield, Leeds and Liverpool have demolished these flats and built conventional housing instead.

Housing and health status

Housing conditions are associated with health status in a number of ways. An obvious indicator is inadequate heating, which can give rise to hypothermia in the old and very young. Overcrowding may cause respiratory diseases and may also contribute to mental illness. The homes of managers and professionals are likely to possess more amenities than those of unskilled workers:

Possession of amenities in the home

	Professional/managerial	Unskilled manual
Central heating	87%	44%
Refrigerator	99%	90%
Telephone	96%	50%
Car	93%	33%

Source: OPCS General Household Survey (HMSO, 1982)

As many as 2 million dwellings in England are considered unfit for human habitation because they lack basic amenities such as showers or bath, or require repairs to them. These dwellings are likely to be inhabited by unskilled workers. They are also likely to be in areas where the air is polluted with industrial waste. One survey of pre-school children carried out in 1977 found one in 10 inhabited dwellings where at least one of the following criteria applied: overcrowding, no separate unshared bathroom, shared WC and no sole use of fixed water supply.

Social improvements have cleared the air of the more visible pollutants such as smoke, removed the most serious contaminants from food and the water supply, and provided for the hygienic disposal of waste. As a result, the diseases that affect people in the past, such as tuberculosis and cholera, have now been replaced by heart disease and cancer.

How can economic factors such as income and unemployment affect a person's development and well-being?

Diet
People with little or no money may not be able to pay for food or heating. Children and older people, in particular, need good, nourishing food for their physical development, such as bone formation.

Leisure
People who have been unemployed for a long time, and who therefore have little money, are just able to buy the necessities for life: heating, food and shelter. They have little opportunity for leisure activities because of the cost. Being unable to take part in leisure activities, buy luxuries or visit friends can lead to depression and possibly ill-health.

Housing

Poorer people are more likely to live in cheap and poor housing and in crowded conditions. Cheaper accommodation is usually found in the middle of cities where the air may be polluted by car exhaust fumes and emissions from factories. Health can be affected by damp conditions and pollution.

Education

Children learn the 'rules' of the society they live in. The process is never-ending – it continues throughout life as we meet new experiences.

The intellectual needs of children are partly met by their time at school. There a child not only improves the skills learned at home, such as eating and drinking, but also learns how to relate to others and develop intellectual skills.

Schools offer linguistic (language) and intellectual stimulation. Children learn how to play and take part in creative activities. These activities will become more ordered as the child gets older, and the child will learn to read and use numbers (numeracy).

Those that stay at school until they are 16 will have the opportunity to obtain qualifications such as GCSEs and GNVQs. Staying at school or college until the age of 18 allows a student to gain vocational qualifications, BTEC or City & Guilds qualifications, or A-levels and GNVQs. These will allow a young person to enter higher education.

When a child is at school, s/he will be influenced by teachers. Think back to your days at primary school. Was there a teacher you liked? Did you work harder for this teacher? If you did, why do you think this was so?

Parents also play a part in the education their children. Early stimulation and the availability of opportunities for personal development provided by parents can make a great difference to a child's academic performance and ability to make personal relationships.

Employment

Some groups are particularly vulnerable to becoming unemployed, such as those on low wages. A survey in 1980 of over 2000 registered unemployed men found that as many as 50% had been receiving the lowest earnings in the national earning distribution. There is clear evidence that there is a high rate of unemployment among young people, older workers, those in poor health and women.

Researchers suggest that the loss of a job is comparable to bereavement. Many unemployed men, for example, experience feelings of hopelessness, self-blame, sadness, lack of energy, loss of self-esteem and self-confidence, insomnia, suicidal thoughts and an increased use of tobacco and alcohol. People react to unemployment in different ways depending on:

- the availability of work in the future
- the individual's feelings about the circumstances surrounding his or her loss of job. (For example, does the unemployed person feel the victim of circumstances and not personally responsible?)
- the response of spouse, children and relatives
- the sense of 'loss of face' or respect in the community
- the financial implications
- the extent of supportive networks in the community.

Many unemployed people experience significantly fewer positive feelings and more strain, anxiety and depression. Becoming employed again very quickly restores well being.

The effects of unemployment upon health, however, are not at all clear. Some US studies have found little correlation (positive relationship) between unemployment and ill-health but UK studies indicate that it may be a factor in poor health. The latter studies found high levels of stress among the unemployed. Unskilled people and those who have been unemployed for long periods tend to have higher blood pressure and also tend to be fatter than those people in the professional class. They are also more likely to suffer from arthritis, angina, respiratory problems, alcohol-related disease and mental illness.

2.3 Common factors that affect health and well-being and the different effects they can have on people

Risk to health – the effects of lack of sleep

When you don't get enough sleep, you are less fun to be with and you may appear dull and lethargic. Different people need different amounts of sleep. Adults average 8 hours a night, older people need less and younger people more.

While we sleep our bodies repair themselves. Good sleep is vital for the processes of renewal in the body. A person who is deprived of sleep experiences great difficulty in concentrating and dealing with even simple problems.

There are two types of sleep. We sleep deeply for about 2 hours then we pass through a stage of lighter sleep, when we dream. During this time our eyes make rapid movements and the brain waves are faster than in ordinary sleep. Both types of sleep are needed. If we are unable to sleep properly, it may indicate that we are worried, depressed, drinking too much or taking insufficient exercise. There is nothing better than natural sleep and people who are experiencing problems might consider some of the following remedies:

- taking more exercise – try walking or jogging
- having a milky drink before bed
- avoiding rich, highly spiced foods
- reading before going to sleep
- trying a mental task like counting sheep
- keeping warm
- cutting down on noise
- not smoking in the bedroom
- having a really comfortable bed.

On some occasions a doctor might prescribe a sleeping tablet as a short-term solution to help a person through a difficult time.

Activity 11

Monitor and record your sleep pattern. For a week note how you react if you do not get enough sleep.

Substance abuse

Cigarettes, alcohol and illicit drugs are used to change feelings and moods. They can cause a lowering of stress levels and enhance feelings of well-being. They are all to a greater or lesser extent addictive and can all cause harm both to the user and others. The use of alcohol and cigarettes are legal and more socially acceptable than drugs. However, there is increasing opposition to smoking in public places and many people regard smoking as antisocial behaviour.

Smoking

Most smokers admit that they wish that they had never started to smoke, not least because of the health risks that they face. It is widely accepted that smoking contributes to over 90% of all deaths from lung cancer and is implicated in many other cancers. Many young people smoke: in 1996 13% of those aged between 11 and 15 were regular smokers. Girls are more likely to smoke (15%) than boys (11%). Children in this age group tended to smoke between 47 and 56 cigarettes a week. Most of these smokers had already become dependent on cigarettes: more than two-thirds said that they would have difficult in giving them up even though 98% said that they knew that smoking caused cancer.

Particular problems include:

- *Lung cancer*. There are 40 000 cases of lung cancer diagnosed in Britain each year. Ninety per cent of these cases are caused by smoking and a large percentage of these people are dead within two years of diagnosis. Lung cancer occurs when the lethal cocktail of chemicals in cigarette smoke attacks the genetic material in the lung cells. This causes changes that make the cells multiply wildly so that they collect together. Masses of cells build up and the lungs cannot work. Smokers are four times more at risk from these cancers, even if they do not inhale.

Bronchitis. This is a serious inflammation of the tubes leading to the lungs. The tubes become blocked by a jelly-like mucus and then the damaged tissue is easily infected by bacteria. Bronchitis can also affect non-smokers, but it is more common and worse in smokers.

Emphysema. This is a lung disease caused by the destruction of the feathery branches deep in the lungs. People suffering from the condition are initially short of breath, but eventually so dependent on oxygen supplies that they can hardly move outside their own home. Nine out of ten cases of emphysema are caused by smoking.

Hardening of the arteries. Another condition associated with heavy smoking is the 'furring up' of the arteries. This makes it extremely painful to walk and can lead to amputation of limbs. Arteries are the tubes that carry blood from the heart. The tubes become 'furred up' when fatty deposits, caused by factors such as smoking and high blood cholesterol, collect. These fatty deposits are called *atheroma.* The presence of atheroma makes it harder to pump blood through the tubes and limits the amount of oxygen that can be carried around the body. The narrowing of the heart's own arteries can result in severe chest pain. A heart attack occurs when one of the arteries is completely blocked by a blood clot and this can kill.

Heart disease. Smoking contributes to 25% of deaths from heart disease. The specific ways in which smoking promotes heart disease are not certain. Nicotine may be involved because it makes the heart beat faster and therefore the heart's requirement for oxygen is greater. It also makes the blood stickier and harder to pump. Smokers also take in carbon monoxide, which reduces the oxygen-carrying capacity of a smoker's blood by as much as 15%. In an attempt to compensate for this loss, the body produces extra haemoglobin, which means that the blood becomes more likely to clot. Carbon monoxide also contributes to the hardening of the arteries. So, smoking goads the heart to beat faster while making the blood harder to pump, more likely to clot and less likely to carry oxygen. Because of the extra pressure smokers place on the heart they run greater risks during and after surgery.

Cervical cancer. Woman smokers are twice as likely to get cervical cancer (cancer of the neck of the womb) than non-smokers.

Miscarriage. Pregnant women, even those smoking less than 20 cigarettes per day, are 20% more likely than non-smokers to miscarry (lose their baby). Premature births and stillbirths are also more common amongst smokers than non-smokers. The same is true for infertility (the inability to have children).

Gum disease. Smokers are more likely to have gum disease and consequently dental problems.

What is 'furring up' of the arteries called?

Passive smoking

The health risks from smoking are undoubtedly heavy. The risks of ill-health, however, are also run by other people in terms of **passive smoking**. People who live or work in smoky atmospheres without smoking themselves are termed passive smokers. They are vulnerable to the same diseases, as explained above, but to a lesser extent. It is very difficult to estimate the risk of passive smoking, but two studies of children with parents who both smoked estimated that the children breathed in the same amount of smoke as if they had actively smoked 80–150 cigarettes per year.

Passive smoking can also aggravate asthma and other bronchial conditions.

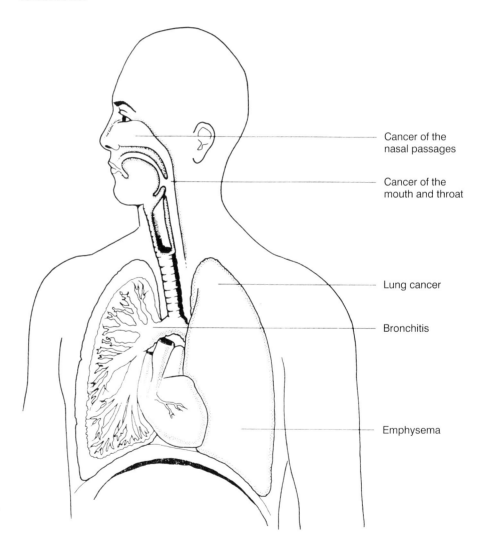

— Cancer of the nasal passages

— Cancer of the mouth and throat

— Lung cancer

— Bronchitis

— Emphysema

Problems caused by smoking

Stopping smoking

It is difficult to stop, but if you do then within one year the health risks you run are 50% more than those of non-smokers. After five years of non-smoking you have little more risk of heart disease than a life-long non-smoker. Most people would like to give up smoking but find it very difficult.

Another reason for giving up smoking is that it has become an antisocial habit. More and more venues are becoming completely smoke-free or have special smoke-free zones. People generally feel that smoking leaves unpleasant smells on clothes, hair and breath. It is no longer considered sophisticated or attractive to smoke.

Finally, smoking is very expensive. It is hard exercise for a smoker to calculate the annual expense of their smoking habit. It is easy too for the smoker to justify the expense by saying that they do without other things in order to afford cigarettes. It does seem ironic, however, to pay for possible damage to your own health.

Smoking is also costly to the community in terms of passive smoking, nursing care and working days lost through ill-health caused by smoking. About half the fires dealt with by the fire brigade are caused by smoking. In 1985, the fire at Bradford football ground, in which 56 people died, was caused by a discarded cigarette. Similarly, in the tragic fire at King's Cross Underground station, the dirt and debris in the escalator shafts were ignited by a cigarette.

How to stop

If you are young and only smoke occasionally, it is worth noting that many heavy smokers started with an occasional, social smoke, once a week perhaps, but the habit became established and very difficult to break.

As smoking is an addiction rather than just a habit, the smoker must really want to stop. It needs a lot of willpower to stop as the smoker will probably feel the effects of withdrawing from the nicotine.

Some people switch to low-tar cigarettes and these do cause less damage. It is difficult, however, for heavy smokers to adjust to the change and some may smoke more because they find that the low-tar cigarettes are less satisfying. in some areas, health promotion councils offer group therapy sessions to support people as they give up.

Few people manage to reduce their level of smoking so low that they stop entirely. The temptation is to creep back up gradually. On the other hand, to 'cold turkey' and stop suddenly is very difficult because of the effects of nicotine withdrawal.

In Britain there are 10 million ex-smokers. It is not easy, but it can be done!

Activity 12

a Discuss the following issues:
  i Is the government doing enough to discourage smoking? (At present there is a partial ban on advertising tobacco products, government health warnings are being displayed and it is illegal for cigarettes to be sold to those under 16 years of age.)
  ii Is it true to say that people have a right to enjoy themselves as they wish?
b Within your own group, ask the smokers how they started and what advice they would give to anyone who is tempted to smoke.
c Why do you think that teenage girls are more likely to smoke than boys?

Alcohol abuse

Unlike smoking, drinking alcohol is still very socially acceptable – the vast majority of adults drink alcohol and consumption has doubled since the 1950s. Indeed it is expected that we will drink on certain occasions. To refuse alcohol may be embarrassing. You may think that people will consider you odd or cranky if you refuse even a mildly alcoholic drink. It is often overlooked that alcohol is in fact a drug. It is a legal, socially accepted drug, but one that can cause much personal and social damage. In fact, there are more deaths through excessive drinking than through heroin abuse.

What is alcohol?

Alcohol is formed by the fermentation action of yeasts on various fruits or cereals. The resulting liquid, with various additions, may be drunk as wines or beers. The alcohol may be further concentrated by distilling or boiling the water off to produce spirits, such as whisky, gin or vodka. Different drinks contain different amounts of alcohol.

Ten grams of pure alcohol, the amount contained in half a pint of beer, is regarded as one unit. This unit measure is the equivalent of one glass of wine or a pub measure of spirits. The table below lists the unit levels of various alcoholic drinks, but it is important to note that:

- wines vary a great deal in strength and it is better to check the label than to assume a particular unit level
- there is also a range of strengths in beers from fairly light beers and lagers, at 2 units per pint, through to stronger ones such as Guinness and Stella Artois, which contain 3 units per pint. Some beers are even stronger.

Unit levels of various alcoholic drinks

Drink	Units
1 bottle of spirits	30.0
1 bottle of table wine	10.0–18.0 or 7.0–12.0
1 bottle of sherry/Martini/port	14.0
1 can of special lager	4.0
1 bottle of special lager	2.5
1 can of beer	1.5
1 pint of cider	2.0–4.0
1 pint of beer	2.0–3.0
1 glass of wine	1.0–2.0
1 glass of sherry/Martini/port	1.0
1 measure (25 ml) of spirits	1.0

Alcohol levels

Current advice is that men ought to consume no more than 2 pints of standard beer or lager per day and women no more than 2 small glasses of wine. This is equivalent to 3.4 units for men and 2.3 for women per day.

When the police stop drivers suspected of 'driving while under the influence of drink', they measure the **blood alcohol concentration –** BAC. This is the concentration of alcohol in the body's system. It is difficult to state precisely how much alcohol needs to be consumed in order for a person to be above the legal limit because people have different tolerance levels in relation to alcohol. As a broad rule, one unit of alcohol or half a pint of beer is equivalent to a BAC of 15 mg (milligrams) per 100 ml (millilitres) of blood. The legal limit for driving is 80 mg per 100 ml BAC, so an average-sized man would be around the

What is the legal BAC level for driving?

legal limit for driving if he has drunk five units or 2.5 pints of ordinary beer (or its equivalent). A smaller man or a woman might be above the legal BAC limit if they had drunk five units of alcohol.

The factors that affect alcohol concentration in the body are:

- the amount of alcohol consumed
- the size of the drinker
- the sex of the drinker (women have proportionately less body fluid than men and are therefore less able to absorb alcohol)
- the rate at which drinks are consumed
- the amount of food in the stomach.

Almost all of the alcohol in a pint of beer is absorbed after one hour if it is drunk on an empty stomach. If there is food in the stomach the alcohol is absorbed more slowly.

Most of the alcohol consumed is removed from the body by the liver. A little is eliminated through breathing and urine. On average, one pint of ordinary beer takes about two hours to filter out of the body.

Drinking habits

In 1996 27% of men over 18 drank more than 21 units per week and 14% of women (an increase from 9% in 1984).

Key Skills

You can use this case study to provide evidence for Key Skills Application of Number N2.1, N2.2, N2.3.

Case study

Alicia Robinson runs a small boutique. The boutique was a thriving concern but high interest rates have meant that recent months have been more difficult. On Friday evening she has arranged a promotion for the boutique to coincide with some new garments arriving from France. It is a cheese-and-wine celebration. So:

- On Friday evening Alicia drinks five glasses of wine very rapidly. 5 units
- On Saturday at lunchtime Alicia meets her boyfriend for a pub lunch. She has half a pint of cider, one sherry and some sandwiches. 2 units
- On Saturday evening Alicia goes to a dinner dance. She drinks two gins and four glasses of wine. 6 units

Plot the level of Alicia's BAC on a graph like the one below. Remember:

- *One unit of alcohol = 15 mg/ 100 ml BAC.*
- *Five units is very near the legal limit.*
- *Two units of alcohol takes about two hours to filter through the body (rough guide only).*

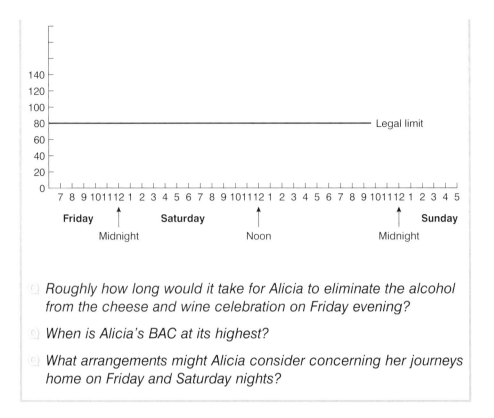

Q Roughly how long would it take for Alicia to eliminate the alcohol from the cheese and wine celebration on Friday evening?

Q When is Alicia's BAC at its highest?

Q What arrangements might Alicia consider concerning her journeys home on Friday and Saturday nights?

How excessive alcohol consumption affects the body

Many people turn to drink in times of stress. Alcohol is a depressant drug that can act as a tranquilliser if amounts below the recommended units are taken. If excess alcohol is taken, however, the nervous system is initially 'weighed down' by the depressant nature of the drug, and then when the effects wear off the nervous system rebounds like a coiled spring. This 'rebound' produces feelings of nervousness, tension and restlessness.

Stomach disorders like gastritis are also common among drinkers. Gastritis is the result of alcohol stripping parts of the stomach of its mucous lining, producing pain and eventually diarrhoea. Peptic ulcers are also associated with prolonged heavy drinking.

In the short term, alcohol may have a positive effect on sleep patterns. In the long term, however, alcohol increases anxiety, depression and therefore insomnia.

Alcohol also has the effect of suppressing the body's own immune system, making heavy drinkers more vulnerable to infection and disease. Alcohol stimulates insulin production in the pancreas. Insulin reduces sugar levels in the blood and can lead to very low blood sugar counts. Thus the person feels drowsy, weak, trembly and may faint. Alcohol can simultaneously increase weight and cause malnutrition.

Alcohol provides calories – one gin and tonic is 150 calories and a pint of beer 300 – but it does not provide nutrition. So you can become quite fat but be malnourished. Some drinkers do lose their appetite and excessive drinkers tend to eat very little so they become extremely thin. A further point in connection with food and alcohol is that alcohol can stop your body absorbing vitamins. The B vitamins are especially vulnerable and in some cases severe brain damage can result from the deficiency of thiamine (vitamin B1).

The effects of alcohol on the heart are complicated. Moderate drinking can lower the risk of heart disease in certain people, but excessive drinking increases the risk.

Continual excessive drinking may cause inflammation of the brain, gradually reducing brain size and resulting in intellectual deterioration. (Note that this is not the same as temporary 'brain muddle' after occasional heavy bouts of drinking.)

One of the best-known conditions associated with heavy drinking is cirrhosis of the liver. Cirrhosis means that the liver is at first enlarged by the continual work that it has to do in dealing with the alcohol. Subsequently, it becomes inflamed and packed with fat. Eventually, it becomes scarred and shrunken so that it can no longer function. A fatty liver can generally become healthy with a nutritious diet and avoiding all alcohol. Alcoholic hepatitis leads to cirrhosis in about 50% of cases, but in itself is not quite as serious as cirrhosis. Cirrhosis kills about 10% of people who have been problem drinkers for 10 years or more.

When you have a drink, you experience a warm glow and that signifies that many of the cells in your body are bathed in ethyl alcohol. If this happens often enough and with sufficient quantities of alcohol, then changes take place in some cells. At times, these changes can be malignant, so heavy drinkers are at a higher than average risk of cancers of the throat and liver.

Some heavy drinkers suffer from **delirium tremens** ('the DTs'). This is a dangerous state of alcohol withdrawal that causes violent tremors, hallucinations, rambling speech and hyperactivity. It usually takes place three to four days after very heavy drinking has stopped. Between 15 and 30% of people with the so-called DTs die. There are several, less severe levels of withdrawal, which come as soon as heavy drinking stops. Some heavy drinkers actually suffer alcohol-induced epileptic-type fits.

It is ironic that media images of drink often portray it as an aphrodisiac (increasing sexual desire and performance). In fact, heavy drinking reduces sexual function in both men and women. Impotence in heavy drinkers is not uncommon.

Activity 13

The calorie count of popular drinks is as follows:

Drink	Calories
1 pint of beer	300
1 glass of wine	80
1 whisky	90
1 vodka and orange	130

a Compare the calorie levels above to those of fruit juices, tea, coffee, slimline tonic and bitter lemon.

b If 10 000 extra calories can produce 1.5 kilos (3 lb) of fat, how much weight would you gain by drinking an extra 2.5 pints of beer each day for a fortnight?

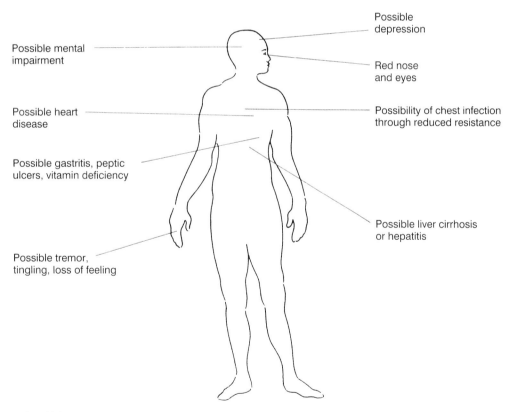

Drink to your health!

The effects of alcohol abuse

- Alcohol is a factor in many road deaths.
- Alcohol is a factor in many criminal offences.
- Alcohol is a factor in much family violence.

It is impossible to record the amount of misery, pain and unhappiness that heavy drinking causes in families.

Alcohol and driving

In connection with road traffic accidents, research shows that, even after only two pints of beer, some people's judgement and co-ordination can be less reliable. After five pints there may be a loss of self-control, more aggression, less balance and blurred vision.

The idea of testing drivers to check alcohol levels was first introduced in 1962, but there was no maximum level fixed at that time. In 1967, the 80 mg/100 ml limit was introduced and the police had the power to stop drivers. In May 1983, a cheaper, quicker way of measuring BAC, with an instant computerised printout, was initiated.

If the results are positive, then the driver is taken to the police station for further tests. In court, the lowest level reading is the one used. If the driver is found guilty then he or she may be disqualified from driving for a year and the licence is endorsed.

Female drinking patterns

During the mid-1960s and 1970s, male alcoholism doubled, but female alcoholism trebled! There are also increasing rates among women of drunk driving and arrests for drunkenness.

There has been a lot of discussion about why women are drinking more. Some suggestions are:

- that women have greater social freedom now than before
- that women have more pressures today in that they may be expected to work both inside and outside of the home
- that more women work and therefore have more financial independence
- that it is now more socially acceptable for women to drink
- that drinks traditionally favoured by women, such as gin, sherry and liqueurs, have actually gone down in price in real terms.

Why do you think more women are using alcohol today?

Whatever the reason, the effects are serious. Women can damage their livers by drinking smaller amounts and over a shorter period of time than their male counterparts. Similarly, women are more at risk from brain damage, certain cancers and ulcers. They become physically dependent on alcohol more quickly than men, so they show withdrawal symptoms earlier.

During pregnancy, drinking is especially dangerous as it can damage the fetus.

Activity 14

Controlling alcohol consumption

Make a list of the reasons why you think people drink. If you drink yourself, then look at the list of reasons below and comment on them in the light of what you have read in this chapter.

- It helps me relax.
- It helps me to feel confident.
- It helps me pull myself together.
- It helps me sleep.
- I like to be sociable.
- I enjoy the taste.
- I find it refreshing.
- I drink out of habit.
- I drink to forget my worries.
- I drink when I am under pressure at work.

Activity 15

Keeping a drink diary

If you are worried about how much you drink or even how much you spend on drink, a useful monitoring exercise is to keep a drink diary.

Record your alcohol consumption every day for about 12 weeks. It may help to use the headings in the Table on page 116 so that you can see if any particular patterns emerge.

Once you have kept your diary ask yourself:

a Did you drink more than you intended to in each case?
b Do you sometimes regret how much you drank the day before?
c Does your drinking ever cause trouble?

Very heavy drinkers are sometimes encouraged to draw up 'troublesome' and 'trouble-free' drink diaries. Obviously, factors like who you are drinking with, how much money and time you spend and whether drinking is the sole activity all affect consumption levels. Below is a list of steps that you might consider if you are trying to reduce your alcohol intake or if you are working with people who are trying to cut down.

How to cut down

Tell people you are cutting down, but be careful, as some may see this as provocation and aim to make you drink more.

115

Date	Sun 4/11/0-	5/11/0-	9/11/0-
Time	12.30–1.30 pm	7.00–10.30 pm	8 pm
Hours spent	1.5	3.5	1.5
Place	'Hammer & Pincers' pub	West End	'Hammer & Pincers' pub
Money spent			
Units consumed	2.5	10	2
Other activities	Darts	None	Cards
With whom	George and Alex	Nobody	George and Alex
Consequences/ how you felt	Quite relaxed; good chat about football	Had awful day at work; drank to console myself; felt very rough Tues am	Good – enjoyed myself

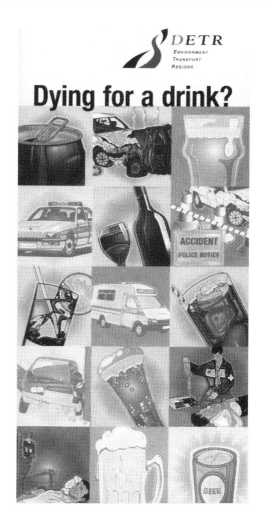

- Start drinking later than you do at present.
  Take smaller sips.
- Put your glass down between sips.
- Occupy yourself, either with an activity or by conversation. Do not take spirits and lager or beer together; you take in alcohol much faster that way.
- Dilute spirits with water or a mixer.
- Eat a meal before you drink.
- Learn to refuse drinks.
- Know exactly how much you have drunk.
- Have some 'rest days' when you do not drink at all.
- Learn to relax without drinking.

Obviously, if people have serious problems then professional help must be sought. People may need help for underlying problems such as bereavement, marital strain or pressures from work. Some psychiatric hospitals run group therapy sessions at alcohol treatment units. In severe cases, people may need to be admitted to hospital for detoxification (allowing all the alcohol to leave the body) or 'drying out'. This does not cure alcoholism but helps to arrest the physical damage caused by it.

Drug abuse

The definition of illegal drugs

Drug misuse means those forms of drug-taking that meet with social disapproval. This includes possession, for non-medical use, of illegal drugs under the Misuse of Drugs Act 1972. Cannabis, LSD, opiates, amphetamines and solvents are all illegal drugs.

Numbers of young people involved with drugs

A survey carried out in 1998 found that one in five of 16–59-year-olds had tried cannabis at some time; of those aged 16–19 over one in three had at some time taken the drug. Asian pupils registered the lowest number who had ever tried drugs.

Studies indicate that problematic drug-taking is worse in cities and in areas of high unemployment and social deprivation. Official statistics demonstrate an overall increase in the number of drug addicts. If drug addicts inject they run a strong risk of contracting **AIDS** (acquired immune deficiency syndrome).

Why people misuse drugs

People take illegal drugs for all sorts of reasons, from curiosity to a search for some form of escape. Studies indicate four main reasons why people take drugs:

- a mixture of curiosity and pleasure-seeking
  encouragement from peers

People who drink more than two cups of coffee or four cups of tea per day will have levels of chemicals in their bloodstream that will keep their 'rate of arousal' at a higher than normal level. Maintaining an artificially high level of arousal will reduce your ability to cope with any additional stress and will keep your body and mind in perpetual tension. When tea and coffee are reduced you may well feel lethargic and slow for a few days. You may even develop a 'withdrawal' headache. The table below shows a list of caffeine indicators. The recommended adult intake of coffee is two cups per day and, for tea, four cups.

Amounts of caffeine in food and drink

Food or drink	Amount of caffeine it contains
1 cup of instant coffee	90 mg
1 cup of filter coffee	200 mg
1 cup of tea (depending on how long you allow it to brew)	40–70 mg
1 can of Coca Cola	40 mg
1 150 g bar of plain chocolate	100 mg
1 150 g bar of milk chocolate	30 mg

quick fire

What is the effect upon the body or mind of drinking over four cups of tea a day?

quick fire

What effect has solvent vapour on the body?

Solvents

Several hundred substances can be used for solvent abuse: glue, paint, petrol and lighter fuel are just a few. The solvent vapours act as a depressant and hallucinations can be experienced when solvents are inhaled.

Accidental death or injury can happen because the 'sniffer' (solvent user) is 'drunk', especially if they are sniffing in an unsafe environment, such as on a roof or near a canal bank. Sniffing to the point of becoming unconscious risks death through choking on vomit. Very long-term use might cause brain damage. The after-effects of poor concentration, fatigue and forgetfulness can become habitual and affect whole lifestyles and opportunities.

It is an offence for shopkeepers to sell potentially dangerous solvents to people under 18 years of age.

Activity 16

a Find out what help is available within your own community for people involved with drugs.
b Organise a display warning people of the dangers of illegal drug taking. You could:
   i check out suitable places to mount the display, for example in the college/school reception area or library

ii contact the Health Promotion Unit of your local health authority for posters and pamphlets

iii research your own information from as many sources as you can, for example, magazines, books, journals, videos and the Internet, and use the computer to word-process and present them well

iv capitalise on the artistic talent within the group – there are bound to be some eye-catching methods of presentation. Make sure all work is correct, neat, straight and well-mounted.

Risks to health and well-being – diet

Does it matter what we eat?

The influence of diet on health has long been recognised. A healthy diet promotes energy and growth and provides the basis for a healthy life. If we want to feel well, stay fit, have good teeth and keep our weight in proportion to our size, then we need to think about the foods that we eat. It is possible to eat nothing but biscuits, chocolates, snack foods and cake for a day or two without feeling too many ill effects. However, if we continued with this type of diet for a longer period we would begin to put on weight, be at greater risk from dental caries and generally feel less fit. Dietary factors play a significant part in deaths from heart disease and some cancers such as cancer of the stomach and large bowel.

The current recommendations for a healthy diet include:

- eating more fibre
- eating less sugar
- eating less fat.

All of these recommendations could be implemented by simple changes in our daily diet.

Activity 17

a Keep a record over three days of all that you eat and drink.

b Interview an elderly person and find out what they normally eat and drink.

Write down the differences between the two eating habits. What do you think are the reasons for the differences?

The basic nutrients

Deficiencies in vitamins and trace elements such as iron also adversely affect health, especially in pregnant women and older people.

The basic nutrients are:

- proteins
- carbohydrates
- fats
- minerals
- vitamins.

List three basic nutrients.

Each nutrient has a particular part to play in the body's function. A variety of nutrients from different foods are necessary to keep the body in good working order.

Protein
This is needed for the growth and repair of body tissues. It is found mainly in meat, fish, eggs, milk and cheese. Vegetarians obtain most of their protein from soya products, nuts, cereals, peas, beans and lentils. The protein allowance should be divided up between all the day's meals.

Protein should be eaten with carbohydrates as the body uses proteins to supply energy if it is short of carbohydrates. This is an expensive form of energy and it also deprives the body of its source of nutrients for growth.

Proteins cannot be stored by the body and protein-rich foods can be expensive, but it is important that every member of the family should have a regular supply. In particular, children need a large quantity of protein as their bodies are growing. Adults need a smaller quantity for the repair of tissue.

Why is protein needed by the body?

Carbohydrates

These give us energy. The main carbohydrates are sugar and starches. Cellulose is also a carbohydrate, but it cannot be digested and is used as roughage (dietary fibre). Starches are of vegetable origin and contain other useful nutrients. Sugar, however, has no nutritional value other than providing warmth and energy, so it is the least useful of fuel foods.

Why are carbohydrates needed in the body?

Fats

These also provide energy. Fats and oils are obtained from plants and animals and are a very concentrated form of energy. If we eat more fats and carbohydrates than our body needs they are stored and this can lead to obesity. The main fats in our diet may include butter, margarine, lard, vegetable oils and cream.

Minerals

This is a large group of nutrients but we only need them in very small quantities:

- iron, which helps to prevent anaemia – this is found particularly in liver and kidney, dried fruits, eggs, spinach and cocoa
- calcium and phosphorus, which give us strong bones and teeth – main sources are cheese, milk and flour
- iodine, which is necessary for the proper functioning of the thyroid gland – main sources are fish, water, milk and milk products
- sodium, which is found in all body fluids and helps in the function of muscles – mainly found in salt and salty foods such as cheese, kippers, ham and bacon
- potassium, which is mainly present in body fluids and, like sodium, is absorbed and excess is excreted through the kidneys – good sources are milk, cheese, eggs, potato crisps, breakfast cereal, coffee and Marmite
- fluorine, which can help to prevent tooth decay – found in tea, sea food, toothpaste and, in some areas, tap water
- zinc, which is mainly present in bones and helps the healing of wounds – found in a wide variety of foods, meat and dairy products

List six minerals used by the body.

Fluorine, iodine and zinc are known as trace elements. Other trace elements include cobalt, chromium and copper.

Vitamins

The four main vitamins that need to be remembered are only available in a limited number of foods. They are divided into two main groups.

- Vitamins A and D are fat-soluble (dissolve in fat) and are generally found in fatty foods.
- Vitamins B and C are water-soluble (dissolve in water) and cannot be stored by the body; therefore daily supplies are needed.

Vitamin A

Vitamin A is sometimes known as the anti-infective vitamin and can be stored by the body to be used when needed. It is found mainly in dairy products, egg yolk, oily fish (such as herring, tuna and salmon) and fish liver oils. A secondary source is orange, yellow or green plants containing carotene, such as carrots and green cabbage. Vitamin A is used by the body to aid growth in children; it helps our eyes to see in dim light; it protects our skin; and it keeps the lining of the throat, lungs and stomach moist.

Sources of vitamin A

Vitamin B

The vitamin B group contains a number of vitamins, all of which are water-soluble.

- Vitamin B1 (thiamine) is found in brown flour, potatoes, vegetables, meat and yeast. Its main use is in the release of energy from carbohydrate foods, as well as maintaining the nervous system and helping in growth.
- Vitamin B2 (riboflavin) can be found in eggs, cheese, milk, liver and yeast products. It plays a role in the growth of children, keeps the mouth and tongue free from infection and keeps the cornea of the eye clear.
- Nicotine acid (sometimes called niacin) is found in bread, cereals, flour, meat and potatoes. Again it is necessary for the growth of children and prevents digestive disorders.

Sources of vitamin B

Vitamin C

Vitamin C, or ascorbic acid, is water-soluble so daily supplies are needed. It is found in citrus fruits, blackcurrants, rose hips, green vegetables and tomatoes. It helps the body resist infection, keeps gums healthy, helps wounds and fractures to heal and ensures a healthy skin. Vitamin C is the vitamin most likely to be lacking in the UK diet. It is very easily lost from food in storage and during cooking. You can only ensure that there is sufficient in the diet by:

- using fruit and vegetables in as fresh a state as possible
- serving fruits and vegetables raw whenever possible
- keeping cooking times to a minimum
- dishing up and serving food immediately
- using the cooking water (stock), which contains dissolved vitamins, for making gravy or sauces.

Sources of vitamin C

Vitamin D
Vitamin D is often known as the sunshine vitamin and, like vitamin A, can be stored by the body. It is found in fish liver oils, margarine, butter, cheese and eggs. It is important in the formation of strong bones and teeth, and promotes growth. This vitamin can also be made by the body itself by the action of sunlight on the skin.

Sources of vitamin D

Water

This is not usually regarded as a food, but it is important in the diet. Every part and function of the body depends on water and it is being lost continuously through the skin, lungs, kidneys and bowels. This water must be replaced and is obtained from the liquids that we drink and the food that we eat.

Nutritional deficiencies

Everyone has different nutritional needs, and some people can cope with nutritional deficiencies better than others. It has been seen that prisoners of war given exactly the same diet suffered a range of effects, from being hardly affected (apart from weight loss) to blindness and death.

The body is able to adapt to reduced food intake, but too little food over a period of time can lead to ill-health through under-nutrition. In extreme cases, as in developing countries of the world, starvation causes stunting of physical and mental development and wasting. Diseases like scurvy and some forms of anaemia are caused by a deficiency (shortage) of certain nutrients or by the body's inability to absorb those nutrients.

In the UK, we may not necessarily have the problem of starvation, but excessive amounts of food can also cause malnutrition (literally, 'bad eating'), which may lead to conditions of ill-health such as obesity, heart disease or high blood pressure. Too much sugar, for example, may cause tooth decay. In poor countries, diets are often low in fat, while in the West we are advised to reduce our fat intake to prevent heart disease. Adults and children over 5 years are recommended to avoid taking in more than one-third of their total energy or calorie intake in the form of fat.

It is useful to check labels on products and prepared foods just to see the amount of fat or sugar in the product. The greatest amount is listed first. There has been some publicity (and disagreement) about certain fats being connected with particular diseases. It is thought that high intakes of saturated fats (lard, suet, cocoa butter) can increase the cholesterol level in some individuals and so increase the risk of heart disease.

Some nutrients are necessary for good health. The possible effects of deficiencies of these nutrients are mentioned below. Don't forget that people have differing needs.

Carbohydrate deficiency

If a person's carbohydrate intake is too low, their protein intake has to be used for energy and so the 'growth and repair' function of the protein has less effect.

Mineral deficiency

Iron
Deficiency of iron can result in anaemia (a decrease in the ability of the blood to carry oxygen to the body's cells). A person with anaemia may feel tired and lethargic and be pale. Anaemia can also arise from a shortage of folic acid and vitamin B12. The absorption of iron from food is generally low, but it is increased when the body's stores are low, as during menstruation.

Calcium
Calcium is the most abundant mineral in the body. Too little calcium in young children may result in stunted growth and rickets (a condition where the bones develop badly and the legs are bowed). The condition is rarely seen in the UK today. Among elderly people, the condition may show as osteomalacia. The main cause of such conditions is lack of vitamin D, which assists the absorption of calcium.

Phosphorus
Phosphorus is found in many foods and it is difficult to have too little. If too much phosphorus is taken in the first few days of life, however, this may produce low levels of calcium in the blood and muscular spasms. Phosphorus is found in cows' milk and that is why babies must only have 'modified' milk, special baby milk or breast milk.

Sodium
Sodium and water requirements are closely linked. Too little sodium may result in muscle cramps.

Salt is present naturally in foods and many prepared foods have a high salt content (check the labels). Habitual high salt intake is associated with high blood pressure. Babies under one year old and people with kidney complaints or water retention problems cannot tolerate a high salt intake.

Potassium

Losses of potassium may be large if laxatives or diuretics (medication to reduce water retention) are used or if the carbohydrate intake level is so low that protein is used for energy. In extreme cases, deficiency of potassium can result in heart failure.

Fluorine

Fluorine is found in tea, sea food, toothpaste and water. The fluorine or fluoride level in tap water varies in different parts of the country. Fluorine can help to prevent tooth decay. Take care, however, because an excess of fluoride can cause the teeth to become mottled.

Iodine

A shortage of iodine causes the thyroid gland to swell and this condition is known as goitre.

Zinc

If a diet is too high in fibre, the zinc in food may not be absorbed and this may affect growth and repair.

More knowledge is needed about the trace elements (fluorine, iodine and zinc). The full effects of deficiencies of them aren't fully understood; neither is it known how one may affect another.

Vitamin deficiency

In general terms, a shortage of vitamins can lead to a reduced resistance to disease and feeling unwell. An excess of certain vitamins can also be harmful. The more specific deficiencies are:

- vitamin A – poor vision and, in extreme cases, blindness. An excess of vitamin A is poisonous
- vitamin B1 (thiamin) – depression, tiredness and, in cases of severe lack, diseases of the nervous system; also beriberi in rice-eating communities
- vitamin B2 (riboflavin) – rarely deficient, occasionally deficiency causes sores in the mouth. Can be destroyed by sunlight, so avoid leaving milk on a sunny doorstep
- nicotinic acid (niacin) – in famine areas this causes pellagra, a condition where the skin becomes dark and scaly when exposed to light
- vitamin C – bleeding from small blood vessels and gums; wounds heal more slowly. Prolonged lack causes scurvy. There is no scientific evidence that a lack of vitamin C means more colds
- vitamin D – rickets and osteoporosis (see Calcium deficiency, above).

quick fire

Which vitamin deficiency can cause depression, tiredness and beriberi?

Health risk – stress

Most people are aware that too much **stress** can endanger your health, but too little stress can also be bad for you. People who have few demands made on them or who have little stimulation may find themselves feeling very tired without doing very much or wanting to do very much. Some people thrive on stress, but others find even a minimal disruption difficult to cope with.

What is stress?

Stress is a response. It is the imbalance between an individual and the demands made of that individual. The term stressor is used to describe the demand. This could be a noise, a task or a thought, which makes the demand that produces a stress response in the individual.

An extreme and sudden stress produces a physical reaction. For example, if you think a child is about to run out in front of a car:

- your eyes and ears receive an alarm signal
- your brain registers the child is in danger and sends messages out along the nerves
- your muscles contract in readiness for action
- the strength of your heart beat increases so blood is pumped more quickly to where it is most needed, i.e. your muscles
- chemicals in the brain set off a number of hormonal changes in your body
- adrenaline is produced
- your hearing becomes more sensitive
- your skin goes pale because the blood has to go elsewhere.
- your breathing gets faster
- your blood pressure rises, carrying oxygen more quickly to the heart, muscles and brain
- your sweating increases
- you may be left feeling faint because the fear causes you to breathe too fast, leading to less blood in the brain.

Interestingly, a similar physical reaction may be felt if somebody you feel quite strongly about actually enters the room where you are.

Reactions to stress

People may react differently to stress or have different reactions at different times. There are three types of reaction. For example, if you are engrossed in a piece of work and some friends call round, you might take a:

- *fight response* – you throw down your pen, open the door muttering irritably that you are busy. This sort of person tends to be the conscientious type, who works hard and finds it difficult to relax. Sometimes a person may suppress the fight response so that they appear to be calm and in control, but in fact they are seething within

129

• *flight response* – you might think to yourself that you may as well take a break and put the kettle on. This sort of person is trying to escape from stressful situations. Such a person tends to be more cautious, may withdraw from stressful situations and pass up opportunities for advancement

• *flow response* – neither fighting nor running away, this is an attempt to go with whatever the current trend happens to be. This sort of person usually stays fairly cool, and may be viewed as erratic and having no fixed values, but is very tolerant.

List two responses to stress.

No one response is better than another. Overuse of one particular response, however, may lead to a fixed, rigid pattern and eventually to a stressed state.

Obviously, the responses outlined here are broad stereotypes, and many people fall between these categories, or may vary from one type to another.

Activity 18

Think of something which might cause you physical stress in the next week and try to monitor your own response to it.

Did you fight or run away? Why? On reflection, do you think that was the best reaction to the situation?

Causes of stress

Stress is a highly individual matter. Different things cause stress in different people. Noisy or hazardous environments, relationships or work may all be stressful. Experts acknowledge that major life changes are generally stressful.

Stress at work

The people who experience stress at work are not always top managers. Shift work can be stressful too. Many jobs may involve working with physical and chemical hazards. Safety measures may make it difficult to have working relationships; for example, it is difficult to have any sort of conversation if you have to wear ear muffs or indeed if factory or construction site noise levels are high.

Another cause of stress at work is relationships. Sometimes seniors may exert unreasonable pressure to achieve tasks in unreasonable deadlines.

Below are listed some of the factors people find stressful about work, which may be very difficult to cope with:

• *Money worries* – Your income is low. You cannot earn more. Your job is not secure.
• *Relationships* – You do not get on well with some or all of your colleagues. You are forced to work with people you do not like.

- *Poor working conditions* – You have to put up with noise, vibration, poor lighting, heat, cold, poor ventilation, danger from physical or chemical hazards, fear of accidents, dirt and grime, long hours of overtime and shift work.
- *Poor administration and company policy* – You get a lot of bother from inefficient administration.
- *Workload* – You have too much responsibility or work to handle or not enough work or responsibility
- *Prospects* – There is no hope of promotion or advancement.
- *Recognition* – No one appreciates what you do.
- *Satisfaction* – The job is boring and you have too much time on your hands or is so demanding you have no time left for yourself.
- *Goals* – You do not feel you can ever achieve or finish anything because the demands are constantly changing.

Signs of stress in the workplace

- High turnover of staff
- High absenteeism
- High illness rates
- High strike rates
- High accident rates

If a job gives satisfaction to and has meaning for those who do it, and if there is pride in the work, then the turnover rates, absenteeism, illness, strike and accident rates are all low. Studies in Sweden have shown that, where workers can arrange their own schedules in consultation with a supervisor rather than doing the same job over and over again, there is far greater interest and satisfaction in the work. Control and variety can also lead to higher standards of work.

What happens if you are stressed?

Extreme stress can cause ill-health, but remember that people have differing stress tolerances and that stress can be prevented and managed.

Physical symptoms

These can include any of the following:

- tension in the muscular system, in the back of the neck or lower back (may result in headaches)
- nausea (feeling sick)
- tension in the jaw – grinding teeth
- diaphragm and pelvic muscles become tense
- throat muscles change, leading to changes in voice or nervous laughter
- if the muscle tension is severe, this can lead to blinking, nervous tics, trembling and shaking
- raised blood pressure
- disorders of the glandular system including excessive sweating, dry throat and difficulty in swallowing

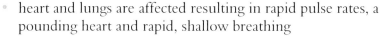

List four physical symptoms of stress.

- heart and lungs are affected resulting in rapid pulse rates, a pounding heart and rapid, shallow breathing
- the nervous system is affected, resulting in dizziness, fainting spells, weakness, lethargy and difficulty in sleeping, too much sleep or disturbed sleep.

Psychological symptoms

These can include any of the following:

- inability to concentrate
- general irritability
- being over-exact
- a sense of mild fear or panic
- inability to enjoy yourself
- inattention to hygiene or dress
- general dullness and flatness – emotional and social withdrawal
- poor work performance
- difficulty in communicating
- loss of sex drive.

List four psychological symptoms of stress.

What can you do to reduce stress?

What can be done to reduce stress? There are many aspects of stress management, but the first is to be aware of your own stresses and reactions to them.

Activity 19

In pairs, work through the interview questions below. One person should be the interviewer and the other the interviewee (the person being asked the questions). You could then swap places if you have time.

Interview questions:
1 Think about something that happened to you that was a very stressful experience for you. Tell me about it.
2 Was this experience something you knew was going to happen or was it a surprise to you?
3 What did you feel when this happened and what did you do?
4 Can you remember doing anything that made you feel any better or less anxious?
5 Did you turn to anyone else for help? What happened?
6 If you had to face this experience again would you do anything different the second time? Could you have done anything to prevent this experience happening or that would have made it less stressful for you?
7 Did you learn anything about yourself as a result of the experience?
8 What factors do you generally find stressful?
9 What helps you to cope with these factors?

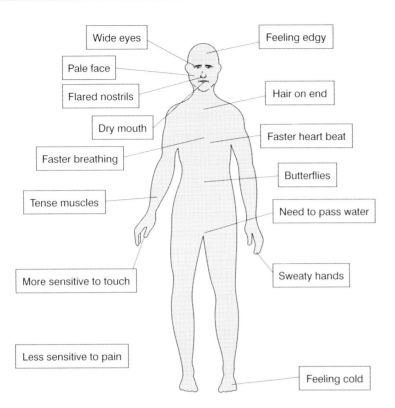

The short-term effects of stress

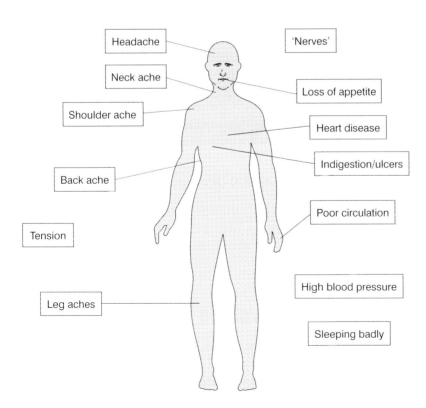

The long-term effects of stress

Groups at risk

The main groups at risk are:

- sexual partners of AIDS sufferers or virus carriers
- homosexuals and bisexuals
- drug addicts
- sufferers from a blood-clotting disorder called haemophilia
- babies born to AIDS sufferers or virus carriers
- prostitutes (both male and female).

However, all sexually active people are at risk if they have several partners and do not protect themselves.

How the virus is spread

Facts about AIDS, HIV and the test

The virus is found in its most concentrated form in the blood and sperm and so any form of sex that involves penetration into the body can spread the disease. Thus all types of unprotected intercourse, that is intercourse without using condoms, can spread the virus. The risk can be reduced but not eliminated if condoms are used.

Needles and syringes shared by drug addicts can cause blood infection. This means that the virus can be passed from one addict to another if they use the same needle or syringe.

Some haemophiliacs have been infected by contaminated doses of a blood product called Factor 8, which is now heat-treated to destroy the virus. In the 1980s a few people were infected through ordinary blood transfusions.

People can actually be 'carriers' of the virus (they are called HIV-positive) without showing signs of the AIDS condition itself. They can knowingly or unknowingly infect other people. The carriers can be healthy for years.

The effects of AIDS

Those who demonstrate signs of the AIDS condition may be ill for between 9 months and 6 years. About 50% die within a year of diagnosis. Once a diagnosis of AIDS is made it obviously has many far-reaching implications, practically, socially and medically, for the individual. First, AIDS sufferers may be refused insurance and mortgages. Secondly, other people may feel that they may also contract the virus and be uncertain about relating to the sufferer. Finally, there is no cure at present for the disease.

Help available

GU (Genito-urinary) clinics:

- can give general advice about AIDS
- can give the HIV antibody test (the test that shows if you are HIV-positive and so have the virus that could develop into AIDS)
- offer special advice and counselling from people who have the virus or AIDS itself. The advice and treatment is free and confidential. You do not need a letter from your doctor. At some

clinics you can just turn up but it is best to phone first to check. The number will be in the telephone directory. If you have difficulty, then phone your nearest main hospital.

The Terrence Higgins Trust, based in London:

- offers help and counselling to people with the virus or AIDS itself, and their friends or relatives
- gives detailed information on what is 'safe sex' and what is 'risky sex'
- gives advice and information to people thinking about having the HIV antibody test.

Your own doctor can advise and arrange for you to have the test.

Other risks to health and well-being – accidents

Living is a hazardous activity!

- Hazards or dangers are all around us.
- At different stages in our lives we are more vulnerable to certain hazards. The old and young are most vulnerable.
- It is important that we can recognise potential hazards.
- More accidents occur at times of peak activity in the day.
- Seasonal factors affect number of accidents.
- Accidents don't just happen. They are usually the result of human, environmental or material factors.

Risks to health and well-being in the home

Every year thousands of people are injured in the home. The most common types of accident involve:

- falls from stairs, ladders, buildings
- bites – from animals or insects

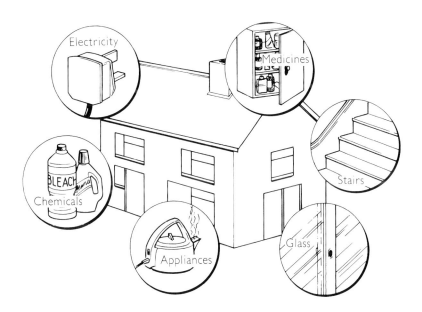

Some hazards in the home

- cuts
- blows – being struck by an object or by a person
- burns, scalds
- foreign bodies
- inhaling poisons
- swallowing poisons
- suffocation
- choking
- accidents involving electric current.

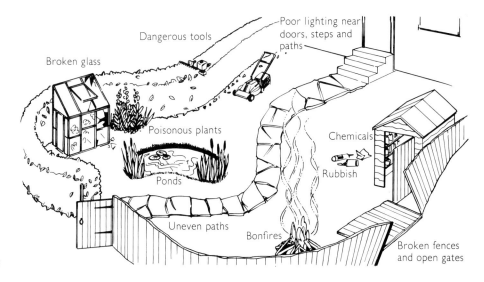

Hazards in the garden

Activity 24

a i Draw a plan of a house.
  ii Divide it into: Kitchen, Lounge/Dining room, Stairs, Bedrooms, Bathroom/Toilet.
  iii On your drawing, note the potential hazards in each room.
b If possible look up Home Accidents Surveillance System 1988 Data UK
  i How many home accidents occur per annum?
  ii Which are the most common types of accident?
c How would a prospective childminder ensure that her house was safe for 3-year-old children in her care?

Poisonous plants

Berries and flowers look attractive and can be a danger to children, who may put them in their mouths.

Activity 25

Find out what plants, berries or flowers can be poisonous to small children.

Unit Two

Road accidents

Road accidents have increased with the volume of traffic using our roads. The effects of an accident are far-reaching, involving the victim, their family and innocent people. Drivers and pedestrians must show responsible behaviour on the roads:

- Be aware of potential dangers.
- Consider other people.
- Be polite.

The most dangerous times on the roads are early morning, evening and between 11.00 pm and midnight.

Drivers and pedestrians should:

- understand road signs
- know speed limits
- know the sequence of traffic lights.

Drivers have accidents when they are:

- not concentrating
- angry
- ill
- driving dangerously, i.e. too fast, in a hurry, too close
- under the influence of drugs or alcohol
- distracted by other passengers
- unable to see properly
- and when they ignore fog, ice and wet road signs.

The law regarding seat belts

- All front seat passengers must wear seat belts.
- All rear seat passengers must wear seat belts where fitted.
- All children under 14 must use a seat belt, child seat or harness where fitted and available.
- A child under 1 year of age in the front passenger seat of a car must use an approved child restraint.

Activity 26

a Find out whether there are any exceptions to wearing seat belts.
b Find out the best type of car safety device for the following:
   i a baby weighing up to 10 kg
   ii a child between 1 and 9 years, weighing between 18 and 36 kg
   iii an older child, 10 years and above.

You can find out this information from your local trading standards office.

Pedestrian accidents
- Pedestrians must behave responsibly.
- Drivers must be aware of the dangers of speed and carelessness.
- Children, parents, teachers and drivers can all co-operate to cut down accidents involving children.

Ways of reducing accidents involving children:

- Introduction of traffic-calming measures
- Educating children once they can understand
- Teaching by rote. By getting children to repeat the Green Cross Code for example, they would then remember it
- Teaching the Green Cross Code.

Cycling hazards
The bicycle is potentially dangerous and is frequently used by inexperienced, untrained riders on busy roads. Serious injuries following cycling accidents include:

- head injuries
- fractured limbs
- severe lacerations and grazes.

Ways of reducing cycling accidents:

- Children should attend cycling proficiency schemes
- Children under 9 years of age should not ride on the road
- Crash helmets should always be worn
- The bicycle should be in good condition and well maintained to BSI standards
- Off-the-road provision and recognition of cyclists' needs by local authorities.

Playground accidents

Although playgrounds are designed for enjoyment many accidents do occur within them. The most common causes are:

- poor design and layout
- over-exuberant (over-excited) children.

Not surprisingly, most playground accidents occur in the summer months.

Equipment most commonly involved in playground accidents includes:

- swings
- climbing frames
- slides
- see-saws
- roundabouts.

Landing on hard surfaces causes many injuries. What can be done?

- Playgrounds should be close to housing to allow safe local play.

- Equipment should be safe and well-maintained, with no sharp protuberances.
- Moving apparatus, e.g. swings, should be sited away from static play areas.
- There should be smaller play areas for under-5s.
- Surfaces should be made of rubber, tree bark or sand, not concrete or tarmac.
- There should be adequate adult supervision.

Playground accident statistics

Activity 27

Visit a playground in your area. Monitor usage of the playground over a morning or afternoon and make notes on the following points:

a How many children use it and of what age groups?
b How much supervision is there?
c What type of equipment is in use?
d Comment on the appropriateness and quality of the equipment.
e Do you think any improvements could be made?

First aid in the workplace

First aid is the immediate care given to a casualty to save life and improve or maintain his or her condition.

Provision for first aid in the workplace is set out in the Health and Safety (First Aid) Regulations 1981. These regulations state that:

- Employers must ensure that adequate and appropriate equipment and facilities are provided for employees/students/residents.
- Employers may also wish to make provision for others visiting the premises, e.g. customers, contract workers.
- Different work activities involve different hazards and therefore different first aid provision is required.

How many first-aiders?

This depends on the types of hazard present in the workplace. In a bank, for example, one first-aider for every 50 workers is recommended. In a more dangerous workplace, more first-aiders are required.

First-aiders must have undertaken training and obtained a qualification approved by the Health and Safety Executive.

Appointed persons

The Regulations state that there should be 'appointed persons' who are authorised to take charge in the absence of a trained first-aider, or where a first-aider is not required, such as in a small, non-hazardous work area. Appointed persons should undergo emergency first-aid training.

Advice and training to deal with specific hazards can be obtained from your local Employment Medical Advisory Service.

The first aid room

The first aid room should contain:

- a sink with hot, cold and drinking water, and disposable cups
- soap and paper towels
- a smooth-topped working surface
- a suitable store for first aid materials
- a suitable refuse container with disposable plastic bags
- a couch with a waterproof surface, clean pillows and blankets.

The first aid box

A first aid box should be made of a material that will protect the contents from damp and dust. It should be clearly identified as a first aid box. First aid boxes and kits should contain a sufficient quantity of suitable first aid materials and nothing else. First aid kits may be provided for particular situations and should be stocked accordingly. An antidote or equipment needed to deal with a specific hazard may be kept near the hazard area or in the first aid box. Sufficient quantities of each, individually wrapped item should always be available.

The Regulations recommend:

Item	First aid box	First aid travelling kit
First aid guidance card	1	1
Individually wrapped sterile adhesive dressings (sticking plasters) in various sizes	20	6
Sterile unmedicated dressings with bandage attached:		
medium	6	
large	3	
extra large	3	1
Eye pads	2	
Triangular bandages	6	
Safety pins	6	2
Individually wrapped moist cleaning wipes	10	6

Where tap water is not available for eye irrigation, sterile water or sterile normal saline (0.9%) in sealed, disposable containers should be provided – at least 900 ml in three 300 ml containers. Where soap and water are not available, individually wrapped cleansing wipes (not impregnated with alcohol) may be used. Disposable drying materials should be provided.

Do not use antiseptic lotions or creams or give any medication. It is advisable to keep blankets, scissors, cotton wool and extra triangular bandages nearby.

The contents of the first aid box should be replenished as soon as possible after use.

In the event of a serious incident the Regulations state that you should:

- treat any injuries
- deal with the immediate emergency
- make premises/machinery safe
- do not destroy evidence required by inspector during investigation
- record injuries in accident book.

RIDDOR (Reporting of Injuries, Diseases and Dangerous Occurrences Regulations 1985)

Failure to comply with RIDDOR is a criminal offence. The Regulations require immediate notification by phone if anybody dies or is seriously injured in an accident at work or if there is a dangerous occurrence.

- A written report must be sent within 7 days to confirm above, and if anyone is off work for more than 3 days as a result of an accident at work
- to report occupational diseases suffered by workers
- to report certain events involving flammable gas in domestic and other premises.

EMAS (Employment Medical Advisory Service)

EMAS is the medical division of the Health and Safety Executive (HSE). It investigates and gives free advice about health at work. You should

What do the initials RIDDOR mean?

contact your local HSE Office or HSE Inspector if you have any queries about health and safety at your place of work. They can supply further information on the Health and Safety at Work Act 1988, regulations and approved codes of practice and first aid.

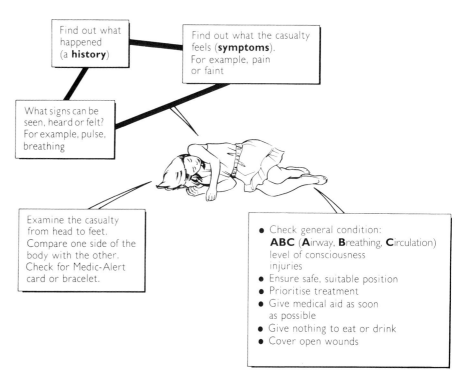

Find out what happened (a **history**)

Find out what the casualty feels (**symptoms**). For example, pain or faint

What signs can be seen, heard or felt? For example, pulse, breathing

Examine the casualty from head to feet. Compare one side of the body with the other. Check for Medic-Alert card or bracelet.

- Check general condition:
  ABC (**A**irway, **B**reathing, **C**irculation) level of consciousness injuries
- Ensure safe, suitable position
- Prioritise treatment
- Give medical aid as soon as possible
- Give nothing to eat or drink
- Cover open wounds

Initial examination and immediate treatment of casualties

Activity 28

a Write a checklist of observations you would make on a casualty who has had a serious accident.

b In groups of two or three, roleplay the examination of a casualty.

c Find out about and make a list of the different types of medical card and Medic-Alert bracelet that are in use.

Health promotion

Advising others on health and well-being

People do not readily respond to preaching and lecturing on health matters so it is necessary to plan carefully.

Unit Two

Why do we draw up health plans for people?

- Empowerment of individuals so that they can make informed choices.
- To bring about changes in behaviour.
- To provide knowledge, and increase awareness, of **health promotion** issues.

Health promotion materials

Health promotion materials help get the message across to people. Selection of appropriate communication channels for the message is crucial. There are two communication channels or ways that help you to get a heath promotion across to other people.

- personal
- non-personal.

Personal communication

Personal communication channels generally provide face-to-face contact. Personal communication allows the message to be individualised and provides opportunities for feedback from the other person.

The effectiveness of personal communication channels is highly dependent on how the other person perceives the persons selected to deliver the message. Highly credible sources are the most effective, provided that they are perceived as having expertise and as being trustworthy and likeable. Such individuals may be perceived as role models. Personal communication channels may be useful when supporting other people in making a decision to improve their health and well-being. The use of peers may also be effective. For example, ex-drug-addicts have been highly effective both in getting the anti-drug message across and in working directly with addicts in order to get them off drugs.

Non-personal communication

Non-personal communication uses no personal contact or feedback. It relies on print media (newspapers and magazines), electronic media (radio and television) and display media (billboards, signs and posters). Non-personal communication channels may be directed at a mass audience (large and undifferentiated) or at specialised audiences.

The objectives of a health promotion campaign

Health promotion campaigns inform individuals about the ways in which their lifestyle choices can affect their health and well-being, and ultimately influence individuals to make different and difficult choices.

All health promotion campaigns should have clearly stated aims and objectives. These specify what the campaign is hoping to achieve: what results are desirable, Objectives should be quite specific and achieved within a specified time period.

New parents

Young love

Consumers

Meningitis C
Reduce the risk
Your guide to the new meningitis C vaccine

NHS

Parents and teenagers

Who is the target of these health campaigns?

It is important that objectives can be evaluated (i.e. have people stopped smoking or lost weight?), so the way in which they are stated is important. They should be as measurable as possible. Objectives should also be realistic and obtainable.

Activity 29

Present advice about health and well-being

In this assignment you are going to prepare a health promotion display for specific client groups. You should divide into groups of three or four to do this. There are several tasks to complete as part of your action planning.

a   In your groups, decide first on the target group you wish to prepare the display for. You will have to take into account the experience within the group, perhaps from placement or voluntary work. It is good to prepare a display for a group with whom you have had contact and whom you know something about. You may decide to present the display to your contemporaries in your class on a topic that affects adolescents. If the small groups within your class prepare displays for children, adolescents, adults and elders then you

▶▶

will have covered all the client groups mentioned in the range statement.

b First think about how to research the possible factors affecting the lifestyle of your chosen group. You will need to look at books on general human development and this Unit of this book. You may be able to find newspaper articles, magazine features, health journals and videos. It would be helpful if you could divide these tasks among yourselves and agree a time to share the information.

c Once you have some background information about your client group, you should decide on a likely health promotion topic. Research the topic you decide on – again using similar sources, including establishments connected with the subject, possibly a Health Education Centre. Again, divide the tasks so that you can compete the research more efficiently.

d When you have gained all the information you can, think about the best methods of display. You will need to present some factual material in an attractive or shocking way to make people take notice. Charts and graphs could be produced on the computer and you may have someone in the group who is good at art! Collecting artefacts can also make a stimulating display – for example, for Dental Health and Childcare, toothbrushes, kept first teeth or a can of Coke are all eye-catching.

e Once this display is set up you should be prepared to give a short talk to the rest of the group to explain what you have done and why. If your display is for children, for example, then it would be appropriate to treat the group as children, using clear language for the designated age group. If you can present the display to real children then this is even better.

f Write a brief report on the impact of the display.

g After the period of the display, make sure you dismantle and return any borrowed items.

2.4 Physical measures that can be used to measure good health

Height and weight

We are all familiar with our own body size and shape. Looking around we can see there is an immense variation in others' sizes and shapes. We are all individuals.

Average or normal?

What do we mean? Always remember, it is possible to be different from the average height, weight, length, etc. but still be within normal limits.

The following measurements are used as a guide to an individual's health and well-being:

- height
- weight.

Weight

The average weight for a newborn baby is 3.5 kg. The largest recorded live-born baby weighed in at 9.3 kg (20 lb 8 oz)!

Babies should be weighed regularly, as weight gain and contentment are signs that they are being fed adequately.

Suggested times for weighing:

- months 1 and 2 – weigh once a week
- months 3–12 – weigh once a month
- over 12 months – weigh at 6-monthly intervals.

A baby can be expected to double his/her birth weight in the first 6 months, and treble it by the end of the first year.

Too fat? Children will become fat if they over-eat and do not have enough exercise. Both children and adults can tend to over-eat if they are worried, bored or insecure. It is unwise to give a small child excessive quantities of sweets or fattening foods. Excessive weight gain in the early months makes it more likely that a child will be overweight in later life.

Height

The average length of a new baby is 50 cm. By the second birthday, a child is likely to have reached half his or her eventual adult height.

The table opposite shows height and weight from birth to 5 years.

It can be dangerous for parents or carers to become preoccupied with a child's size. If a child is happy, contented, growing and energetic there is nothing to worry about.

Peak flow/lung volume

The measurement of air taken into and expelled from the lungs is spirometry. Changes in lung volumes provide the best measurement of obstruction to air flow in the respiratory passages.

A spirometer consists of a hollow drum floating over a chamber of water and counterbalanced by weights so that it can move freely up and down. Inside the drum is a mixture of gases, usually oxygen and air. Leading from the hollow space in the drum to the outside is a tube that has a

Average heights and weights – birth to 5 years

Age	Weight		Height	
	kg	lb	cm	in
Girls				
Birth	3.4	7.5	53.0	20.9
3 months	5.6	12.3	–	–
6 months	6.9	15.2	–	–
9 months	8.7	19.2	–	–
1 year	9.7	21.4	74.2	29.2
2 years	12.2	26.9	85.6	33.7
3 years	14.3	31.5	93.0	36.6
4 years	16.3	35.9	100.4	39.5
5 years	18.3	40.3	107.2	42.4
Boys				
Birth	3.5	7.7	54.0	21.3
3 months	5.9	13.1	–	
6 months	7.9	17.4	–	
9 months	9.2	20.3	–	
1 year	10.2	22.5	76.3	30.0
2 years	12.7	28.0	86.9	34.2
3 years	14.7	32.4	94.2	37.1
4 years	16.6	36.6	101.6	40.0
5 years	18.5	40.7	108.3	42.6

mouthpiece through which the patient breathes. As s/he inhales and exhales through the tube, the drum rises and falls, causing a needle to move on a nearby rotating chart. The tracing recorded is called a spirogram.

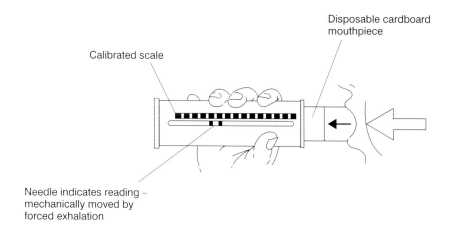

Calibrated scale

Disposable cardboard mouthpiece

Needle indicates reading –
mechanically moved by
forced exhalation

Mini peak flow meter

Various measurements are made of lung capacity. Vital capacity refers to the volume of air breathed out after a person has breathed in as fully as possible. The normal capacity is approximately 2500–3000 millilitres (ml). It is higher in males than females. Forced vital capacity measurements are taken in the form of peak flow measurement.

Vital capacity is reduced in obstructive lung diseases, such as bronchitis (inflammation of the bronchi, the large air passages in the lungs). A person suffering from asthma would also have a reduced vital capacity, due to difficulty in breathing because of muscular spasm of the bronchi.

Activity 30

If possible, obtain a mini peak flow meter from your teacher. This is a small, tube-shaped structure with a calibrated measuring scale and disposable cardboard mouthpieces for the purpose of preventing cross-infection. The more basic versions are fairly inexpensive and can be obtained from sports equipment suppliers. They are frequently used as part of fitness assessment testing. Mini peak flow meters are simple to use. You should inhale and then forcibly and rapidly exhale into the mouthpiece. Normally, the 'best of three' readings is recorded.

Compare readings with your friends.

Safety point: Ensure safe practice. If you or any of your friends experience any pain or discomfort as a result of this activity, stop immediately and seek medical advice. Ensure that you use a new disposable mouthpiece for each person, in order to avoid the risk of cross-infection.

Resting pulse rate and recovery after exercise

Measuring the pulse
Each time the heart beats to pump blood, a wave passes along the walls of the arteries. This wave is the pulse and it can be felt at any point in the body where a large artery crosses a bone just beneath the skin.

The pulse is usually counted at the radial artery in the wrist or the carotid artery in the neck.

Taking a pulse
The finger tips (but not the thumb tips) are placed over the site where the pulse is being taken. The beats are counted for a full minute and then recorded. Normally the rhythm is regular and the volume is sufficient to make the pulse easily felt.

The three main observations made on the pulse are:

- rate
- rhythm
- strength.

The average adult pulse rate varies between 60 and 80 beats per minute, while a young baby has a heart rate of about 140 beats per minute.

An increased pulse rate may indicate recent exercise, emotion, infection, blood or fluid loss, shock and heart disease.

Body mass index

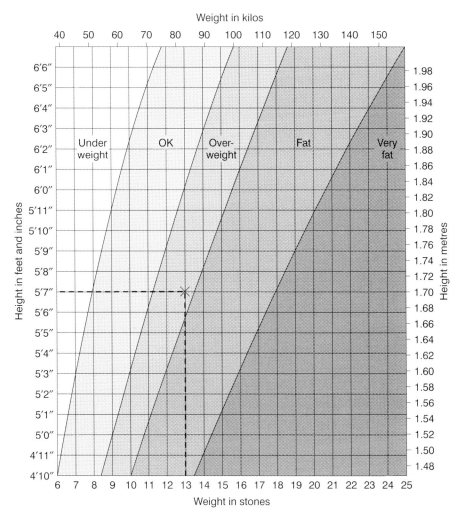

(For example, a person who is 5′7″ tall and weighs 13 stones is overweight)

This is a graph showing the heights and weights of adults. To find out whether you need to lose or gain weight, draw a line up from your weight and across from your height. Put a cross where the two lines meet

---

Activity 31

Measuring physical fitness

There are many tests that have been devised to measure physical fitness. Many involve detailed measurements and calculations. This activity will give you some idea of the level of exercise that will help you to improve your health.

▶▶

Warning: Do not attempt to carry out this activity if you know you have any breathing difficulties or heart disease. The activities are not dangerous, but it would be best to get medical advice about exercise routines.

a Work with a partner so that you can measure each other's pulse rate. You will need a watch with a second hand. Together decide what you consider to be gentle exercise. (This may be as simple as walking steadily upstairs.)

b Before you start, measure your resting heart-beat by counting the heart-beats for 15 seconds using the pulse found in your wrist. Multiply the answer by four to get the beats per minute. Record this figure as resting pulse.

c Carry out your gentle exercise for 1 minute. Then record your heart-beat at 1-minute intervals until it gets back to the resting rate.

d Repeat the activity for longer periods of 2, 5 and 10 minutes (or possibly longer) until it takes more than 5 minutes for your pulse to return to its resting rate.
The last but one exercise level is the amount of exercise you should start off doing. The heart rate achieved is a guide as to the level you should work to.

e Using the result as a guide, start a programme of exercises three or four times a week. At the end of each exercise session, measure your maximum heart rate and the time taken to return to the resting rate.
Increase the amount of exercise to reach your maximum pulse that still returns to normal after 5 minutes' rest. You should find that you are able to exercise more as you get fitter.

Note: The maximum heart rate that you should not exceed is calculated by subtracting your age from 220:

220 – your age = maximum heart beats per minute.

It is unlikely that you will approach this with the gentle exercises, but you should try to double your heart-beat during exercise.

Key terms

After reading this unit you should be able to understand the following words and phrases. If you do not, go back through the unit and find out, or look them up in the Glossary.

Health and well-being	*Aerobic*
Nutrition	*Anaerobic*
Diabetic	*Pulse rate*

Economic factors   Vitamins
Self-esteem   Stress
Substance abuse   Personal hygiene
Passive smoking   AIDS
Blood alcohol concentration   Health promotion
Delirium tremens   Nutrient
Carbohydrates   Safe sex

Test yourself

1 List five factors that affect the health of an individual.
2 What do you understand by the word 'lifestyle'?
3 List three benefits of taking regular exercise.
4 List four health problems associated with smoking tobacco.
5 List five ways in which excessive drinking of alcohol affects the body.
6 List three reasons why people misuse drugs.
7 What help is available for drug users?
8 Give three recommendations for maintaining a healthy diet.
9 What is the average adult pulse rate per minute?

Assignment

Produce a plan for promoting health and well-being for one person who is at risk.

Your plan *must* include information about risks to health, two measures of health, time scales and targets for improvement and also supporting health promotion materials.

To gain a merit or distinction you are asked to analyse certain situations or tasks. Analysing means breaking the task down into detailed parts – if you are to analyse the way in which health promotion material supports a plan for promoting health, you would explain in detail your reasons for saying that the material supports the plan.

Tasks

1 Choose one person and identify factors that affect their health and well-being – consider physical factors and at least one social or economic factor.

2 Clearly explain factors that cause potential risk to the health and well-being of your chosen person.

Get the grade

To get a **PASS** you must complete tasks 1–5

To get a **MERIT** you must complete tasks 1–8

To get a **DISTINCTION** you must complete tasks 1–10

3 Correctly use and report measures of health and well-being that reflect the needs and abilities of your chosen person (is s/he a child, adult or elderly person?).

4 Communicate your plan to the chosen person. Do this in a form that they can understand and clearly explain how the targets in the plan can be met.

5 Chose from a number of health promotion materials information appropriate to the plan and explain why they were selected.

6 Analyse how your chosen person's measures of health could be affected by a range of risks and factors such as financial constraints, social pressure or self-esteem.

7 Prioritise the long and short targets with time-scales of your plan and give reasons for the targets chosen.

8 Analyse the ways in which the health promotion material you have chosen supports your plan.

9 Consider the physical, social and emotional effect on your chosen person of achieving the targets you have set in your plan.

10 Anticipate potential difficulties in achieving the plan and propose realistic ways that they could be overcome.

Key Skills — Opportunity

	You can use this Assignment to provide evidence for the following Key Skills
Communication C2.1a, C2.1b, C2.3	Discussing/presenting the plan to a specific person
Communication C2.2	Identifying health promotion materials
Communication C2.3	Producing a plan
Application of Number N2.1, N2.2, N2.3	Using measures of health

Understanding personal development

What is covered in this unit

At the end of this unit you will be asked to produce a report on **human development** based on one or more case studies. If you would like to see further details of the tasks you are likely to need to carry out for assessment please refer to the end of the unit where an assignment has been set (see pp. 194–5). This unit will guide you through what you need to know in order to successfully put together this report. You will be assessed on this work and awarded a grade. This grade will contribute to the overall grade you will get for Unit Three.

Materials you will need to complete this unit

- Case studies
- Information from health and social care workers (health visitors, etc.)
- Development charts (supplied in this unit)

3.1 Personal growth and development

Have you ever thought about why you are the way you are – why you are you? What has influenced your well-being or otherwise? Can you help being like your parents? Can you work through or avoid some of the factors you don't like about your parents for yourself? Would it matter, in terms of health, which side of the city you were born in or at which end of the country? Is good health simply a matter of looking after yourself or are there other factors which come into play? Such questions and others are tackled in this unit.

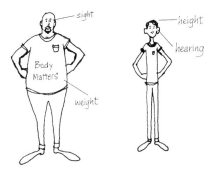

Although these factors may be studied separately, they are in fact all related. Generally, people in good physical health also feel positive and relate well to others. As their personal feelings are good, they probably tackle educational issues confidently and become successful. Conversely, if someone has a lot of illness, it is quite easy to become emotionally low and be less enthusiastic about work and relating to other people. Factors are inter-related – so that if you are physically hungry, it is difficult to concentrate on your assignment!

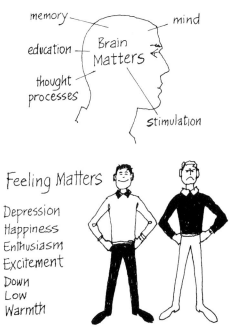

It is impossible to say how far we are the way we are because of what we have inherited genetically or because of what we have learned. Is a child intelligent because of his/her genetic make up or because of a stimulating, encouraging home? Is s/he born intelligent or made intelligent? There is no definite answer to this question.

Characteristics of development in different stages of life

The factors that affect personal development are given in more detail at the end of this section.

As individuals we are changing and developing throughout our lives. Everyone develops at different rates so that, when comparisons are made between babies, allowances are made for individuality. If, however, a child or baby was assessed to be considerably behind his or her contemporaries then other investigations would need to be carried out.

The development process is made up of alternating periods of rapid growth (often accompanied by disruption in life – 'hassle') and periods of relative calm, or consolidation. There are times when the changes pile up or when one central change affects the entire system, such as when we start school. Often these changes in role are accompanied by big changes in language and thinking, so that a child starting school, for example, may seem a bit distant until s/he adjusts. They may even revert to old habits, such as thumb sucking. Relationships need a new pattern and it is best to keep other changes to a minimum at such times. Familiar foods, leisure patterns, rooms and decoration all help to gain consolidation in the period of transition or change.

Summary of the stages of human development

Infancy
0–2 months

- Child mainly behaves in an instinctive, reflexive way – cries for food or if in pain.
- Begins to smile, may show interest in the world around.
- Probably no clear-cut attachment to a single individual.

2–8 months

- Child now coos and babbles.
- May show preference for one adult over another.
- Vision improves, can sit up and reach for things.

8–18 months

- Child learns to crawl and walk.
- Can use a series of actions to gain what s/he wants.
- Speaks words and half sentences.
- Will show attachment to care givers and an interest in other children.

18 months–2 years

- More complex language.
- Transition time (time of moving from one stage of life to another) – possible disruption of sleeping and eating patterns.

2–6 years

- Motor skills (walking, using hands, etc.) are refined.
- Co-ordination improves so that games of bat and ball become fun.
- In terms of thinking, the child can use words or images to stand for things, develops a gender awareness, can put things into groups and can take other people's perspectives into account.
- Strong attachments to primary care-givers, especially if under stress (child always calls for Mummy or Daddy if frightened or under pressure).
- Play choice may begin to be with the same gender and be for traditionally gender-related toys – little boys may want trains, etc.
- Early friendships formed, evidence of sharing, generosity and aggression.
- Explores further from own base – growing independence.

Early childhood
6–12 years

- Physical growth steady until puberty. Girls may see the beginning of puberty.
- Gross motor skills (riding a bicycle, climbing, jumping, etc.) improve – mountain bike for Christmas!
- In terms of thinking, the child can subtract, order, add up, etc. and can perform tasks in the mind, e.g. silent reading and mental arithmetic.

- Friends or peers become important, usually same gender.
  Individual friendships become more important. Attachments to
  parents less obvious, but still very much needed. Continues to
  absorb gender roles.

Adolescence
12–18 years

- Puberty is completed in this period. Increase in physical strength
  and speed.
- Most adolescents can reason morally – what is right and wrong,
  and why.
- Need to seek out future career, as well as interest in opposite
  gender.
- A lot of conflict as peer pressure mounts, possibly against parental
  influence.
- Questioning of taught values, roles, ideas, mood swings,
  depression, elation.

18–21 years

- No significant physical changes.
- In relationships, idea of giving and taking is consolidated – mature
  response.
- Understanding that identity is a complex product of past
  experiences and background.
- Intimate relationships, possibly new self-concept through work;
  religious and political views may be worked through.

Adulthood
22–40

- Physically most people function at the maximum before the end of
  this stage, similarly with mental performance.
- Socially – possible marriage, parenthood, work peak.

40–65

- Physically and mentally, possibly some loss of ability.
- May be demands from children and ageing parents.
- Marriage may be reassessed, friendships may increase in
  importance.
- Mid-life physical and emotional upheavals will occur in the early
  part of this stage.

Old age
65–

- Further decline physically and mentally.
- May experience loss of social contacts and gradual withdrawing or
  'disengagement', cutting off from wider issues.

- Retirement. Readjustment to post-retirement phase.
- Family may be more significant in terms of mutual help.

The ageing process and its effect upon personal development

Ageing starts with **conception** and depends on the mother and father's genetic and social status and on a whole host of acquired and environmental factors (external influences such as housing, where you live and where you work). It is not yet fully understood why people age. Health in middle age, and attention to physical fitness, diet and early treatment of disease may prevent much illness in old age.

Old age is sometimes discussed not as a stage in life but as a problem of residential care, social amenities or medical attention. It is as if society sees the arbitrarily chosen age, 60 or 65, as the period when people cease to be ordinary members of the community and become a special group for whom the whole community has to make provision. We sometimes now talk of the 'young old' (65–74) and the 'old old' (those over 75 years of age).

Why has the social impact of old age become more important?

The social impact of old age becomes important because of the increasing proportion of old people in the community. The number of people over pensionable age in 1996 was 10.7 million and the numbers are set to grow, to 11.8 million in 2010 and 14 million in 2021. At the beginning of the 20th century only one person in 21 was over the age of 65. By the year 1996 this had risen to 18% of the total population (just over one in six), more of them women than men. Women can expect to live longer than men and they also tend to have less serious health problems than men.

The transition from adulthood to old age receives little recognition. One reason may be that the onset of old age is gradual and we cannot pinpoint when it actually occurs. Many elders have feelings of regret and reluctance during this period and are not eager for public acknowledgement of their change of status.

Most people have to retire from work when they reach retirement age and this may bring about changes in their personal development.

Health
Retirement has no adverse effects on physical health; in fact in some cases a person's health may improve. Many people retire because they are in poor health and this may account for the idea that people die or become ill a few weeks or months after they retire.

Income
At retirement most people experience a reduction in income and those without a private or company pension may experience a big drop in income as the state pension becomes worth less and less.

Social relationships

Withdrawal from the labour force does not automatically result in a reduction of social contacts with families, friends or neighbours. The more contacts you have before you retire the more you are likely to have after retirement.

Marital relationship

When a spouse retires the other partner must adjust their daily routines to the other's presence. Retirement may mean that a couple can attain greater companionship. Some couples find, however, that retirement puts a strain on the relationship.

Support for the elderly

There are two implications of the increasing numbers of elderly people in the community. There will be proportionately fewer younger **carers** and there are going to be more infirm and unfit elderly people to look after. Over 25% of elderly people have no children to support them. Nearly one in three of the over-75s have no family member to support them.

3.2 Social and economic factors that can affect personal development

Social class

Social class is a form of social stratification system for putting people into strata (layers). In the UK, the Registrar-General, a government official, collects data on all births, deaths and marriages, and census data every ten years.

What does the Registrar-General do?

Since the beginning of the 20th century, the Registrar-General has grouped people into five social classes, from a list of 20 000 jobs, as a way of classifying people. The groupings are based on the income, status, skill and educational level of each job.

Classes 1–3 are what we would usually call the middle class and Classes 4–5 might be termed working class.

The five social classes – the Registrar-General's classification

	Class		Examples
Middle class	1	Professional	Doctors, dentists, solicitors
	2	Managerial	Managers, teachers, nurses
	3	Non-manual	Clerks, typists, travel agents
		Skilled manual	Electricians, hairdressers, cooks
Working class	4	Semi-skilled manual	Postmen or women, farm workers
	5	Unskilled manual	Cleaners, labourers

The Registrar-General's classification has been criticised because:

- It does not take account of unemployed people.
- It does not take account of people (usually women) at home looking after children or dependent relatives. It is based on the male's occupation so that if the wife/female partner has a job in a higher class, it doesn't count.
- Some occupations don't fit easily into categories and there are lots of grades within individual occupations.
- Individual occupations may be up- or downgraded in society before this is reflected in the scale.
- People are classified by occupation – but people's lifestyle does not necessarily follow a national middle-class pattern because they are teachers in a middle-class bracket.
- The scale doesn't necessarily reflect the power base. The people at the top don't have any more power than those at the bottom. If the refuse workers went on strike, life could become very difficult.

The government's new social classification system

Why did the government change the classification system?

In September 1998 the government introduced a new **classification system** to meet the criticisms of the old system, which had so few classes. The changes were necessary because most of the population now considered itself middle class. The old system introduced in 1921 had failed to take account of the shift towards office work and the service industries. Under the new system doctors, dentists and solicitors have slipped from the top class to the third, below the Queen and owners and managers of large companies.

New classification system

Class	Examples
1	The Queen, large company owner
2	Company executive, manager of 25 people or more
3	Doctor, lawyer, scientist, teacher, librarian, IT engineer
4	Policemen, nurse, fire-fighter, prison officer
5	Sales manager, farm manager
6	Office supervisor, civil servant, lab technician
7	Computer operator, dental nurse, secretary
8	Small business owner with under 25 employees, publican
9	Self-employed bricklayer, driving instructor
10	Factory foreman, shop supervisor, senior hairdresser
11	Craft and related workers, plumber, mechanic
12–17	+ other classifications + (Un)skilled or unemployed

Case study

The Jones family live in a fairly spacious semi-detached house in a residential area. Mr Jones is a successful solicitor. Mrs Jones is a dentist – she works part-time. They have two children aged 9

and 11. Mr and Mrs Jones are keen to keep fit, they jog regularly and they are careful about their diet. As a family they enjoy horse-riding and they have recently bought a horse of their own. They are all in good health at the moment, although there is a history of coronary disease. Mr Jones's father died at the age of 50. His mother lives alone in Winchester. Mrs Jones's parents also live in Winchester.

Think about the family described in the case study and discuss it in terms of the family's potential health and well-being. Try to put the family in a social class bracket. Give reasons for your choice and comment on the usefulness of the new classification system.

Carry out some research in your library in connection with social class and health. Inequalities in Health, a government report produced in the 1980s, is a useful book to look at.

Income

Economic factors like the amount of income we have and how we spend it affects how we live, and is linked to social class.

Activity 1

There is a great difference between the income level of a person in the top 5 classes and a person in Class 10 or 11. What possible differences might there be between two such people in the following areas:

a diet?
b health care?
c housing?
d leisure?
e education?
f holidays?
g paying for help with house maintenance?
h paying for help with house cleaning?
i paying for help with house or gardening?
j paying for help with child minding?
k paying for help with catering?
l stress levels?
m occupational hazards?

Of course, there are individuals in the higher classes who lead very unhealthy lifestyles and the opposite may be true for people in the lower classifications.

Once you have made this comparison you may be able to think about a scenario with greater extremes. If a person is unemployed, for example, this heightens the difficulties and the need.

In education, research has shown that children lower down the social scale tend to do less well educationally than those higher up. Consider for yourself the differences there might be between the groups in terms of role models (people to base yourself on), encouragement to go on to higher education, private education, extra tuition, a place to study and believing you can do it because you are expected to achieve.

What is a role model?

Housing and environment

A home is a very significant factor in an individual's life. The place where we live can affect not only our physical health but also our mental health, and can even affect us socially. The effects are even greater if an individual doesn't have a home!

Activity 2

In small groups, consider the possible implications of living in bad housing, cramped, damp conditions or temporary housing for the following people:

a a single parent with young children
b an elderly person living alone
c a teenager living with his or her family.

Don't forget to consider the physical, emotional and social aspects of their lives. Think also about what addresses mean – not just as places where people live but as saying something about them. The community that they come from may send messages to other people who may make assumptions about them.

Housing standards have improved a great deal in the UK since the end of the Second World War, but just over 5% of housing is still considered unfit and homelessness is an increasing problem.

In 1991, 70 000 people had their homes repossessed. This means that they could not afford to repay their mortgage so the building society had to reclaim the property. Sometimes people's businesses fail and their home is reclaimed by the bank or building society as part payment for the money initially borrowed.

Why do people who are homeless have bad health?

The number of people who have to live in temporary accommodation is rising. This is unsatisfactory for the households concerned because they feel insecure and unsettled. Thousands of people have no home, possibly because they have personal difficulties like alcoholism or mental health problems. Whatever the reason for their homelessness, one thing that is certain is that once they begin to live rough their health declines rapidly. The average age of death for a homeless person is 47 years.

Work

List four jobs that may cause potential health problems.

Working conditions can affect health. Think of the risk factors involved in building, refuse collection, working in steel factories or with heavy industrial equipment.

There is no doubt that the higher up the social scale you go the better your life chances are in terms of health, education, career opportunities and personal well-being.

Lifestyle choices – socio-economic groups

Some people argue that those in the lower **socio-economic** groups have worse health because of their habits, such as drinking, smoking and poor diet. People in the north, for example, have been accused of eating too many stodgy foods. This sort of comment is not helpful because it blames the victim for the situation they are in rather than looking at wider issues such as poverty, which is often the root of many problems to do with lifestyle. The comment could be described as a deficit model, one that makes the victim out to be deficient in some way. 'Asian mothers don't know enough about childcare and that is why the mortality rate (death rate) of Asian babies is so high' is another example of a deficit model statement. Further questions might be asked about what makes people lower down the social scale smoke or drink. What pressures are on them to resort to these things? What alternatives have they? Limited income often means limited lifestyle.

People from ethnic minority groups may find it more difficult to obtain the health care they need. Information may not be available in community languages, transport may not be available to attend hospital appointments or the demands of other children may make it impossible to sit in long queues for antenatal checks. Similar points could be made concerning white people from lower class groups.

Activity 3

Discuss the following questions and statements. Summarise your discussions for your file.

a Why might a child from a lower socio-economic group be five times more likely to be killed on the road than a child from Class 1 or 2 (old classification)?

b Why is the perinatal mortality rate among Asian people very much higher than among white people? (Perinatal mortality rate means the number of babies who die in their first week of life.)

c Why are two-thirds of the students at universities from middle-class backgrounds?

d Children from lower social classes suffer more respiratory infections and diseases, ear infections, squints, and are likely to be of shorter stature than their middle-class counterparts.

e Mortality rates for people from Class 5 are sometimes twice as high as for adults in Class 1 (old classification).

f Black people are more likely to be diagnosed as schizophrenic than white people.

Further information on the effects of negative lifestyle choices can be found in Unit Two.

Relationships – family and friends

How early are relationships formed? Early! No one really knows how early a baby notices its mother, father or main carer. The significant point is that if a child is denied positive early relationships for a long time, this will affect his or her development. Babies who are neglected or ill-treated, who have had little stimulation, eye contact or physical contact, need a lot of help to become bright and affectionate themselves. Similarly, as the child grows, the relationship that develops gives him or her a pattern for future relationships.

Influences on health and well-being

The influence of parents

Psychologists such as Freud, Bowlby and Piaget hold that a child's early relationship with its parents (particularly the mother) sets the tone of later relationships. Children with secure relationships with their parents are more likely to be accepted by their peers (friends, contemporaries). Sometimes children who have difficult relationships with siblings (brothers and sisters) form closer friendships outside the home.

You can use Activity 4 to provide evidence for Key Skills Communication C2.1a.

Activity 4

Discuss the following questions with your class colleagues and summarise your conclusions:

a   Can parents help their children to be accepted? If so, how?

b   What makes some children bully?

c   Why are some children bullied? Are some children more vulnerable to bullying than others? Why?

d   Can parents influence their child's behaviour if he or she is a bully?

e   Can teachers prevent bullying?

f   Can parents assist their child to develop strategies to cope or deal with bullies?

g   What effect might bullying have?

The influence of the family

Although the relationship between parent or main carer and child is a central one, other early relationships soon become significant. The relationship between brothers and sisters may be tempestuous at times, but they do affect development.

Activity 5

a As a class, discuss the following questions:
Are you an only child? An elder child? From a large family?
The youngest child? How do you think this may have
affected your development?

b How much contact did you have or do you have with your
grandparents? How has this affected your outlook?
Summarise your discussions for your file.

In some cultures the extended family (a family that includes
grandparents, aunts, cousins) is very much alive. Today, in British society
the nuclear family is more the norm. This family consists of a couple and
their children living alone. Relatives, in many cases, are a long distance
away from the nuclear family. This is because people tend to move to
jobs away from parents and grandparents.

Activity 6

Discuss and write down what you think are the advantages in
terms of relationships of:

a the extended family
b the nuclear family.

Why relationships?

People differ greatly in their need for close, informal or even formal
relationships. There are those who like to spend long periods by
themselves with no one else to be responsible for or share their company.
Most people, however, need both informal family relationships and more
formal ones to thrive and be happy.

Activity 7

Think about the relationships that exist in a family situation:

a child–parent
b sibling–sibling
c man–woman.

Write down the physical, intellectual, emotional and social
reasons for each relationship.

Clues to help you with relationship (a) child–parent:

Physical:
- for child – food, warmth, care, protection, provision of accommodation, care when ill
- for parent – creation of child satisfies physical need/urge to reproduce. At one time children would eventually provide for the physical needs of their parents as they aged, but this is less common now.

Intellectual:
- for child – parent provides stimulation toys, may assist educationally
- for parent – may see child-rearing as an intellectual challenge.

Emotional:
- for child – parent provides love, security, affection, guidance, calmness
- for parent – child provides joy, hope, satisfaction, pride, someone to love and the pleasure of returned love. The parent will feel glad to be needed and loved.

Social:
- for child – parent may provide direction, opportunities, encourage friendships and introduction to wider relationship
- for parent – child may provide a role, a purpose, a new way of enjoying the social events of life such as Bonfire Night. Child may provide opportunities for parents to make a new circle of friends with other parents and carers.

Try to tackle (b) and (c) on your own, giving physical, intellectual, emotional and social reasons for participating in these relationships.

Formal or work relationships

It is particularly important in social care work that relationships among staff and with clients are positive. Studies show that poor relationships at work are not good in terms of production or efficiency. Poor relationships or non-existent relationships at work can lead to personal dissatisfaction, depression and ill-health. Many people would say that after the financial incentive to work the next incentive is the company of their colleagues or workmates.

Activity 8

a Think about why you want to work in social care. List your reasons in order of importance to you.

b Discuss this list with your class colleagues. Are your reasons the same – have you all placed the reasons in the same order of importance?

Think about your own experience at school: how significant are/were your relationships with your friends in terms of your motivation to attend school and learn?

Teachers too need to form relationships with the groups and individuals they teach to make learning effective.

Social, informal relationships

Often, we participate in relationships because we enjoy them. We may use our leisure time to play football or badminton. We may go to clubs and discos to meet with friends who are unassociated with work or family. This is because we need to gain a balance in our lives. We need to be free from the responsibilities of home and work for a short time to reinforce a lighter side of ourselves. We go to confirm aspects of ourselves that are sporty, fun-loving, creative or even silly.

Activity 9

Interpersonal relationships

Using the text, write a brief report analysing your own relationships. Indicate which relationships are formal or informal and how these relationships have changed. (Some relationships may begin formally but become informal, as when you meet a girl/boyfriend.) Include family relationships.

People who have religious beliefs often like to meet together to share thoughts and discussion, worship and praise. This again reaffirms their faith for the individual. One has to be very single-minded to maintain religious belief in isolation.

If people leave their home town or community and live abroad or in another part of the country, they are often glad to meet with someone from their home town or country while they are away. Why do you think this is?

Family matters: the role of the family in the development of individuals

Parenting is a two-way process. It would be easy for parents if their children simply followed whatever their parents wanted them to do. Children, however, have personalities and wills of their own so it is an interactive (two-way) process. Two children in the same family can be very different even if their parents have brought them up in roughly the same way.

Activity 10

As a class, discuss the following questions and summarise your discussions for your file.

a Does the gender of the child affect the way parents react to him or her?

b Does the position in the family affect the way parents handle children? Think of the eldest and youngest child and how their development may be different because of how their parents have brought them up.

c Are some babies or children more difficult to care for than others? Might this affect parental responses and subsequent development?

d In what ways might babies and children exert influence over adults?

3.3 Self-concept

What is self-concept?

Self-concept means the image you have of yourself – how you see yourself. Some people have a very realistic concept of who they are and what they are capable of. Most of us have an ideal self-concept – someone who we would like to be or be like. It helps in terms of being content if your ideal concept isn't too far from your actual self-concept. It is useful to try to understand something of your own identity or self-concept in caring because it will affect what you say and do in relation to others.

What influences self-concept?

Our self-concept is formed by how people behave towards us and then our response to them. It is a two-way process. We have an image of who we are, and we choose our friends because they are similar to us and like the things we do. In return, they reinforce aspects of our personality that are like them.

They confirm what we are – 'Birds of a feather flock together, not out of luxury but out of necessity'.

A major influence on our self-concept is our primary carers or parents. They help to form our values, attitudes, patterns of behaviour and roles. They are one of the main agents of socialisation.

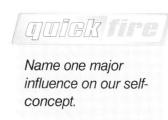

Name one major influence on our self-concept.

What is socialisation? What is its effect upon self-concept?

Socialisation is not socialising – you may do that at discos. Socialisation is a sociological term that is more significant than just socialising – it affects every individual.

Socialisation is the process whereby we become members of society. We are born with instincts to eat, to rest, etc., but we are taught manners, how to dress, language, etc. We absorb our cultural patterns through our parents, friends, education, media and work.

Socialisation starts when we are born and only ends when we die. We are continually being socialised by the new situations we meet in our lives.

Look at the case study below and remind yourself of how your parents have affected your own development. Page 173 also deals with family relationships and how they affect the individual.

Case study

James is 11 years old. He has just finished junior school. He is a tall, healthy-looking boy with blonde hair and pale blue eyes. He has a perfect set of evenly-spaced, white teeth, which are displayed by his frequent grins and smiles. He is old for his school year – his birthday is in September so throughout his school life so far he has been physically and educationally ahead. He is good at sport and plays for the school football team and county tennis. His parents support him totally. They help him with any school work he has in the evenings and transport him to his many sporting events. His mother takes particular pride in buying his attractive, up-to-the-minute clothes and makes sure his tennis outfits are always immaculately laundered.

At school his favourite subject is mathematics. His teacher says he is better than she is at maths, but he is also pretty good at English, science, geography and history. He is often so far ahead that he helps the others and they think he is really good.

Each year a prize is awarded in the school to the girl and boy who have made the most contribution to the school. The staff of the school vote for who they think should gain the prize: James won.

Ⓠ *Do you think James has a positive or a negative self-concept? This is also a judgement on the level of his self-esteem or how he rates himself. Write down also why you think his self-concept is positive or not, giving specific reasons.*

Ⓠ *When you have considered the first question, think about the following and write down your answers.*

a *How many friends do you think James will have?*

b *How do friendships and popularity affect self-concept? How do you feel if you know you are liked?*

c *How will James face the transition to his new secondary school? What attitude will he have?*

d *Educationally, how do you rate his chances in the long term?*

e *If you feel you are good at a particular subject, does this affect your motivation to work at that subject?*

f *If you are good at one subject, what sort of attitude might you have towards other subjects?*

g *What sort of relationship do you think James has with his teacher in the junior school? How will this affect his self-concept?*

h *At home James is very much loved and his parents are proud to have such a son. What difference does this make to James? (Think about what James might lose if he was badly behaved for some reason – would it be worth James risking the loss of his parents' affection?)*

i When questions are asked in class, James often puts his hand up and gives a correct answer. Would it matter very much to him if he gave a wrong answer in terms of embarrassment or loss of self-esteem?

j How do you think James's physical capacity in terms of his height and sporting prowess affect his self-concept?

Roles – what are they?

We learn our **roles** through the socialisation process. We absorb by watching, listening and imitating how we should be, what we should say, how we should act. We learn very quickly what is appropriate. Each situation has its own norms, or guidelines to behaviour, so that when we first go to school we might rage and kick because we don't want to go. When we reach secondary school we still might not want to go, but we tend not to rage and kick because we know the norms of the situation.

Think of other norms

Think of other norms or guidelines to behaviour associated with:

- eating out in a restaurant
- going to church
- dating
- queuing for a bus.

People who don't follow the norms for whatever reason may appear odd, funny and, in extreme cases when they don't follow a legal norm or a law, may end up in court. For example, if we do not obey the speed limit we may end up being fined.

Particular groups have their own norms as part of their culture. There are the traditions of dress, ceremonies, festivals and the norms of table manners and courtesy.

People who are interested in music may have norms that belong to that group. Can you list them?

Norms and roles may change because of factors in society (for example, the availability of contraception changed the role of women) and because of influences on health and well-being and individual development. Sometimes, particular roles are associated with different social class groupings (see below). This isn't very helpful in that it becomes easy to stereotype people because of the social class groupings they are in.

How did the availability of contraception change the role of women?

'You can be my friend, you can be in our gang'

Research shows that it is only when children become less egocentric – that is, concerned with themselves – at the age of about 6, that they develop stronger friendships. Once children are 7 or 8 they are in roles which unfortunately are extremely difficult to break.

Androgyny

Another aspect of popularity and positive self-concept concerns androgyny. This means a child's ability to perform in both gender roles. Those who don't adopt specific male or female roles entirely tend to be more popular and have higher self-esteem.

Other common factors among popular children in school include:

- being friendly
- being outgoing
- being the youngest child rather than the oldest
- success in school
- being physically attractive
- often being tall
- often being good at a specific task activity, for example sport.

Key Skills

You can use this case study to provide evidence for Key Skills Communication C2.3.

Case study

Rachel is 11 years old. She is a county badminton player and enjoys travelling over the country with the rest of the team to play badminton. Once she played an important match with a broken arm – in plaster – after she had fallen over playing rounders. She won the match. She likes clothes and hairstyles, but is quite casual about her appearance and far too interested in sports to spend very much time on traditionally girly matters.

Why is Rachel so popular?

Key Skills

You can use this case study to provide evidence for Key Skills Communication C2.3.

Case study

Tony is also 11 years old, but he is young for his year and small for his age. He has an eyesight problem, which makes some sports more difficult. He often feels frustrated because he isn't good at sport and needs to lash out and kick something or someone because he is angry. On non-uniform days in school Tony's mum said he would just have to go in his uniform because he didn't have anything decent to wear. He hated that day. Everyone asked him if he had forgotten non-uniform day. Tony's dad left home when he was little. Tony still sees his dad but sometimes when there is an arrangement to go to his dad's house, his dad rings up at the last minute to say he is busy and can't see him.

Tony's teacher finds him awkward and negative. She says he is sullen, bad tempered and that he doesn't seem bothered about his work. His test scores are quite low. Tony knows his marks are low and that his work is messy. He feels that he is a failure and that's just the way things must be.

▶▶

What comments would you make about Tony's self-concept?

How would you rate his popularity in the class?

What impact might Tony's father's apparent reluctance to see him have on him? (Some children are abused by their parent(s) – physically, emotionally or sexually. What effect do you think this might have on self-esteem?)

What significance would you attach to Tony's appearance and clothing?

How would you rate Tony's chances of educational success? Would he be one of the ones to put his hand up to answer a question? Why? Why not?

How might Tony be making his teacher's life more difficult? How easy is it to rid yourself of the label of 'trouble-maker'?

What does the final statement of the case study indicate about Tony's feelings of powerlessness to change his situation?

The passage implies that Tony's family is short of money. What other issues in Tony's life might this affect?

If the children of the school Tony goes to are not particularly short of money, if they are from a more middle-class or affluent culture, how might Tony's problems be highlighted and what effect will this have on his self-concept?

What could be done to help Tony improve his self-image?

Activity 13

This is a sensitive activity and is probably best carried out with someone you know well. If you are hesitant about this activity omit it and simply answer the questions at the end by imagining what it is like to be someone from a different culture living in Britain.

Choose someone who is of a different culture from your own to interview. Ask them if they mind answering questions that are about them personally. Ask them the following questions:

a How does your culture differ generally from the culture in Britain?
b What specific differences have you noticed or been aware of in terms of family life or habits and customs?
c Did these differences ever really matter – at school or socially?
d How did these differences make you feel?

You might now find it helpful to read the section, in Unit One, on the effects of discrimination.

The impact of different life events

Life event (in the last two years)	Crisis unit score
Death of spouse or partner	100
Divorce	73
Marital separation	65
Jail term	63
Death of close family member	63
Personal injury or illness	53
Marriage	50
Fired at work	47
Made redundant	45
Marital reconciliation	45
Retirement	45
Pregnancy	40
Change of health of family member	39
Sex difficulties	39
Gain of new family member	39
Business readjustment	39
Change in financial state	38
Death of close friend	37
Change to a different line of work	36
Change in number of arguments with spouse or partner	35
Mortgage over £10 000	31
Foreclosure of mortgage or loan	30
Change in responsibilities at work	29
Son or daughter leaving home	29
Trouble with in-laws	29
Outstanding personal achievement	28
Wife or female partner begins or stops work	26
Begin or end school	26
Change in living conditions	25
Revision of personal habits	24
Trouble with boss at work	23
Change in work hours or conditions	23
Change in residence	20
Change in school	20
Change in recreation	19
Change in religious activities	18
Change in social activities	17
Mortgage or loan less than £10 000	16
Change in sleeping habits	15
Change in number of family get-togethers	15
Change in eating habits	15
Holiday	15
Minor violation of the law	11

Finally, the person begins to reorganise their sense of self and their life in accordance with the new situation and this is very positive.

How we cope with change

Sometimes people try very hard to get over the shock of redundancy or becoming disabled and repress feelings of anger and frustration. This is referred to as a defence mechanism. Research shows that it is best to allow the grief, the tears, the sobbing, particularly with children, because it is part of the healing process. The 16-year-old girl who loses her sight through a brain tumour has got to grieve for the loss of her sight; she has got to mourn all that is no longer available to her before she can begin to work on mobility or learning braille. Repressing the grief may cause many more deep-seated, psychological problems later.

It has been said that people who suffer great loss never really completely readjust, they just go through the motions of everyday life, and that may be true for some people.

In some cultures, it is more accepted to demonstrate grief and bereavement rituals may be more extensive. Families and friends in all cultures support the grieving relative, but in some cultures there is more open, affectionate evidence of this support.

3.5 The type of support available to people

How to manage change

Despite the possibility of positive outcomes, change is often resisted by individuals. Resistance to change, or the thought of the implications of change, appears to be a common phenomenon. People seem to be naturally wary of change.

Resistance to change

Resistance to change may take a number of forms:

- *Selective perception* – An individual's own perception of stimuli presents a unique picture of the 'real' world and can result in selective perception. This can lead to a biased view of a particular situation that fits comfortably into the individual's own perception of reality. For example, lecturers may have a view of students as irresponsible and therefore oppose any attempts to involve them in decision-making about their own learning or course organisation.
- *Habit* – Individuals tend to respond to situations in an established and accustomed manner. Habits may serve as a means of comfort and security. Proposed changes to habits may be resisted.

Activity 18

a How does the family provide support for its dependent members?

b What services exist in your area to help families to look after their members?

What could be the consequence of a lack of social support in a person's life?

There is a body of knowledge that suggests a lack of social support, such as practical assistance, financial help, information and advice, psychological support and close social or emotional relationships, can increase vulnerability to illness and disease. In one study, those who were classed as socially isolated were two to three times more likely to die than those who were part of an extensive social network. Other studies show that disabled people with few social contacts were more likely to deteriorate in physical functioning than people with high levels of contact with others. The main contribution of social support would seem to be that of a buffer, particularly when people are experiencing adverse life events.

Support in the home

Services in the client's own home should provide support with tasks to enable the client to live as 'normal' a life as possible by providing help with:

- Domestic and household tasks
  - cleaning
  - laundry
  - preparing meals
  - shopping
  - collecting pensions
- Personal assistance with daily living activities
  - dressing/undressing
  - washing
  - bathing
  - eating and drinking
  - taking to the toilet
- Emotional and social support
  - conversation/listening
  - company
  - reading, writing
  - accompanying on outings
  - helping to keep in touch with neighbours, etc.

Any support in the home should be co-ordinated and provided with the assistance of other carers, neighbours or friends, and be delivered in a way that fosters independence and realises the care values discussed above. These services should be reliable, co-ordinated, flexible and sufficient to meet the client's needs.

Ways in which clients and their carers can take control of care services

How can people be encouraged to take control?

People should be encouraged to take responsibility for their own lives, which involves choosing which services they want and taking decisions about their lifestyle. This assumes that they will be able to take risks to maintain their freedom and independence. Services should be delivered in a manner that respects the dignity and value of the individual. Services that are offered should be appropriate to the individual's situation, culture and lifestyle.

Information

People need information and knowledge of the services provided. The government encourages agencies to publish details of services available. In order to make informed choices individuals must therefore have adequate information about services and also about complaint procedures. This information should be accessible to all and produced in appropriate languages and formats. The National Health Service and Community Care Act 1990 requires social service departments to provide 'information accessible to all potential service users and carers, including those with any communication difficulty or difference in language or culture, setting out the types of community care services available, the criteria for provision and services, the assessment procedures to agree needs and ways of addressing them and standards by which the care management system will be measured'. This is done by publishing a Community Care Plan and also by setting up consultation procedures with clients and carers. Booklets and leaflets are also used to provide information.

Key terms

After reading this unit you should be able to understand the following words and phrases. If you do not, go back through the unit and find out, or look them up in the Glossary.

Life stages	*Self-concept*
Human development	*Informal relationship*
Conception	*Socialisation*
Social class	*Roles*
Classification system	*Life events*
Socio-economic	*Carers*

1 Explain self-concept.
2 Explain role concept.
3 What are the functions of the family?
4 Explain the term 'deficit model'.
5 What is a norm?
6 Explain what is meant by 'time of transition'.
7 Explain the difference between informal and formal relationships.
8 What is socialisation? Give examples.
9 What is the Registrar-General's classification?
10 What criticisms may be made of this classification?
11 What are the possible implications of social class position?
   Does it matter what class you are in? Why?

Assignment

Produce a report on human development based on one or more case studies. You may use case study material or you can arrange to interview a person of your choice. Remember to make sure that any person that you interview has enough life experience to allow you to present the appropriate evidence.

To gain a merit or distinction you are asked to analyse certain situations or tasks. Analysing means breaking the task down into detailed parts – if you are to analyse positive and negative effects of relations, you would examine in detail these effects.

Get the grade

To get a **PASS** you must complete tasks 1–3

To get a **MERIT** you must complete tasks 1–6

To get a **DISTINCTION** you must complete tasks 1–8

Tasks

1 Illustrate that you understand physical human development by describing the physical characteristics of the five life stages.

2 Describe the social and emotional factors, which affect the development and self-concept in the case study (or person that you have interviewed.) It would be helpful to give examples.

3 For the person you have chosen (or the case study) describe the relevant support that was or could have been provided through their life stages.

4 Show how physical, social and economic factors can affect a person's personal development and self-concept. For example you could show how poverty might affect the ability to buy healthy foods and the possible effects on development and self-concept.

▶▶

5 Analyse positive and negative effects of personal relations on a person's development and self-concept. It would be helpful if you gave examples from the different life stages.

6 Give examples of support provided to a person to enable you to show how this support can assist them through expected and unexpected life changes. For example, what would be the effect upon a bereaved person if they had no relatives or friends to talk to?

7 Discuss the one factor you think has had the most significant influence on the development and self-concept of the person you have interviewed (or the case study).

8 Analyse the different ways in which people cope with changes and how these changes could affect the type of help and support they might need.

Key Skills Opportunity

	You can use this Assignment to provide evidence for the following Key Skills
Communication C2.1b	Produce the report and give an oral presentation to your class
Communication C2.2	Producing the written report

Appendix

Physical, intellectual, emotional and
social aspects of personal
development

Age	Physical factors	Intellectual factors	Emotional factors	Social factors
At birth The new-born baby	An average new-born baby weighs about 3.5 kg and is 50 cm long. Compared with other new-born animals, at birth a human baby is a helpless creature and its growth is very slow. Certain primitive reflexes are present, and these usually disappear by the time the baby is 3 months old and is beginning to make conscious movements on his or her own: • sucking reflex • swallowing reflex • rooting reflex – if one side of a baby's cheek or mouth is touched gently, the head will turn in the direction of the touch • grasping reflex – the fist clenches if an object is placed in the palm • Moro reflex – arms and legs are flung out and then drawn inwards in response to being startled • stepping reflex – if the front of a leg is brought into contact with the edge of a table, the baby will raise a leg as if to 'step' up • walking reflex – if held upright, with the soles of the feet on a flat surface, and moved forward, the baby will respond by making 'walking' steps.			
1 month The infant	Holds head erect for a few seconds. Eyes follow a moving light.	Interested in sounds.	Cries in response to pain, hunger and thirst.	May sleep up to 20 hours in a 24-hour period. Stops crying when picked up and spoken to.
3 months	Eyes follow a person moving. Kicks vigorously.	Recognises carer's face. Listens, smiles, holds rattle. Shows excitement.	Enjoys being cuddled and played with. Misses carer and cries for him/her to return.	Responds happily to carer. Becomes excited at prospect of a feed or bath.
6 months	Able to lift head and chest up supported by wrists. Turns to a person who is speaking.	Responds to speech. Vocalises. Uses eyes a lot. Holds toys. Explores using hands. Listens to sound.	Can be anxious in presence of strangers. Can show anger and frustration. Shows clear preference for mother's company.	Puts everything in mouth. Plays with hands and feet. Tries to hold bottle when feeding.
9 months	Stands when supported. May crawl. Gazes at self in mirror. Tries to hold drinking cup. Sits without support.	Tries to talk, babbling. May say 'Mama' and 'Dada'. Shouts for attention. Understands 'No'.	Can recognise individuals – mother, father, siblings. Still anxious about strangers. Sometimes irritable if routine is altered.	Plays 'Peek-a-boo'. Imitates hand clapping. Puts hands round cup when feeding.
12 months The toddler	Pulls self up to standing position. Uses pincer grip. Feeds self using fingers. May walk without assistance.	Knows own name. Obeys simple instructions. Says about three words.	Shows affection. Gives kisses and cuddles. Likes to see familiar faces but less worried by strangers.	Drinks from a cup without assistance. Holds a spoon but cannot feed him/herself. Plays 'Pat-a-Cake'. Quickly finds hidden toys.
1.5 years	Walks well, feet apart. Runs carefully. Pushes and pulls large toys. Walks upstairs and tries to join in with nursery rhymes. Picks up named toys. Enjoying looking at simple picture books. Builds a tower of 3–4 bricks. Scribbles and makes dots. Preference for right or left hand shown.	Uses 6–20 recognisable words. Repeats last word of short sentences.	Affectionate, but may still be reserved with strangers – likes to see familiar faces.	Able to hold spoon and to get food into mouth. Holds drinking cup and hands it back when finished. Can take off shoes and socks. Bowel control may have been achieved. Remembers where objects belong.

Age	Physical factors	Intellectual factors	Emotional factors	Social factors
2 years	Runs on whole foot. Squats steadily. Climbs on furniture. Throws a small ball. Sits on a small tricycle and moves vehicle with feet.	Uses 50 or more recognisable words: understands many more words; puts two or three words together to form simple sentences. Refers to self by name. Asks names of objects and people. Scribbles in circles. Can build a tower of six or seven cubes. Hand preference is obvious.	Can display negative behaviour and resistance. May have temper tantrums if thwarted. Plays contentedly beside other children but not with them. Constantly demands mother's attention.	Asks for food and drink. Spoon feeds without spilling. Puts on own shoes.
2.5 years	All locomotive skills now improving. Runs and climbs. Able to jump from a low step with feet together. Kicks a large ball.	May use 200 or more words. Knows full name. Continually asking questions, likes stories and recognises details in picture books. Recognises self in photographs. Builds a tower of seven or more cubes.	Usually active and restless. Emotionally still very dependent on adults. Tends not to want to share playthings.	Eats skilfully with a spoon and may sometimes use a fork. Active and restless. Often dry through the day.
3 years	Sits with feet crossed at ankles. Walks upstairs using alternating feet.	Able to state full name, sex and sometimes age. Carries on simple conversations and constantly questioning. Demands favourite story over and over again. Begins to understand sharing. Can count to 10 by rote. Can thread wooden beads on string. Can copy a circle and a cross. Names colours. Cuts with scissors. Paints with a large brush.	Becomes less prone to temper tantrums. Affectionate and confiding, showing affection for younger siblings.	Eats with a fork and spoon. May be dry through the night.
3–5 years The pre-school child	Continues to perfect physical skills, including running, walking, climbing, riding a tricycle, sitting cross-legged, moving in time to music, playing ball games.	Begins to speak grammatically, recounts recent events accurately, enjoys jokes. Starting to gain control in writing and drawing. A recognisable person may be drawn, or a house with windows and a roof. Pictures are coloured neatly. Begins to understand rules of games and idea of fair play.	Needs companionship of other children. Begins to develop personal relationships. Gradually becoming more independent from parents. Plays with other children and by self. Will comfort playmates, choose friends.	Can dress and undress self. Make-believe play.
5–10 years The school child	Taller and slimmer. Features have more adult look. Movements well co-ordinated. Physical skills increase. Growth rate steady, but slower. Girls tend to develop more quickly than boys.	Improved ability to concentrate on one task and finish it. Starts school – structured activities to help child gain knowledge and skills.	Beginning to develop self-image and sense of identity. Growth of feelings about others. Special friendships start to develop. Some may be excluded.	Range of contacts grows when school starts. Influences now include teacher and other children. A child who is used to a lot of individual attention may find it difficult to adjust to school.

Age	Physical factors	Intellectual factors	Emotional factors	Social factors
11–18 years The adolescent	Start of puberty – physical changes as a result of increased production of sex hormones (oestrogen in girls; testosterone in boys). Growth spurt. In girls, breast development, pubic and armpit hair, broadening of hips, redistribution of fat, menstruation. In boys, deepening of voice, pubic, chest and armpit hair enlargement of penis, scrotum and testes, broadening of shoulders, ability to ejaculate. Possible spots.	Thinking more about self and what others think of them. Begins to compare real world with the ideal world, in terms of family, politics, religion. Starting to think about future – job, career, further education.	Mood swings and feelings of ambivalence. Difficult time for adolescents and parents. May seem to be rebelling, but by challenging ways of behaving, they are testing and developing their ideas of what is right and wrong.	Starting to take an interest in the opposite sex. Problems of shyness, embarrassment prevent socialising and inhibit the forming of new relationships.
18–64 years Adulthood	Physical development complete at about 20 – at physical peak. 30+: changes occur slowly and become more apparent in old age (see below). Main period of reproduction for women around 20–40 years. Menopause can start at any time after mid-30s. Ill-health more common later in adulthood.	18–25: may still be in full-time education or starting work, learning new skills. 25–40: possibly for career progression – new challenges.	Coming to terms with new role in work, as married person or partner, as a parent, or as carer of older parents. May experience problems with loss of grown-up children, dissatisfaction with work/ redundancy/early retirement.	Starting new relationships at work, and college, possibly settling down as a couple. Relationships with children and later grandchildren. Social activities probably less when bringing up family and increase again later.
65+ Old age	Changes which occur throughout adulthood become more obvious: skin becomes dry and wrinkled; hair growth slows, may thin, turns grey; long-sightedness may develop; side vision narrower, cataracts and glaucoma possible; hearing, smell and taste less acute; gum disease and tooth decay, lungs, heart, digestion, urinary system less efficient; high blood pressure; muscles less flexible; poor mobility due to arthritic disease; reproduction no longer possible in women, but still possible in men. Body more subject to degenerative disease, e.g. atheroma, osteoarthritis, brain degeneration, cancer.	Ability to learn new things slows down, does not imply less intelligence. Memory may be less reliable. Relieved of employment, may take up creative activities.	Problems may occur as a result of loss of status after retirement, loss of work relationships, loss of partner due to bereavement, change of role as grandchildren born, possible loneliness, isolation, role reversal as may become dependent on others, reduced income.	

Glossary

Aerobic

Exercise that works the heart, lungs and blood system, such as running, fast swimming and fast cycling

AIDS

A disease that results from contracting HIV (Human Immune Deficiency Virus). The HIV virus causes the body's immune system to break down so that it is unable to prevent a person from becoming ill or contracting disease

Anaerobic

Exercise that concentrates on stretching and flexing the muscles, such as yoga and general stretch work

Antidiscriminatory practice

A term used to describe how people seek to reduce discrimination

Blood alcohol concentration

The concentration of alcohol in the body's system

Carbohydrates

Basic nutrients that give us energy. The main carbohydrates are sugar and starches

Care value base

Care values are principles, standards or qualities which are considered worthwhile or desirable by the care profession, and which should be applied by workers in their day-to-day practice

Carers

People who informally help the client, for example a parent, child or neighbour

Classification system

A system of grouping people according to the job they do. Since the beginning of the 20th century, the Registrar-General has grouped people into five social classes. The groupings are based on the income, status, skill and educational level of each job. In September 1998 the government introduced a new classification system to meet the criticism of the old system, which had so few classes

Code of practice

A body of guiding principles to set standards for good practice, for example The Patients' Charter

Communication skills

Skills developed during the use of verbal or non-verbal skills – for example, skills such as talking, writing and drawing

Confidentiality

The right of clients to have information about themselves kept private. You should never breach confidentiality unless what is told to you would involve you breaking the law, or is information that would lead you to believe that the client is going to harm themselves or others

Delirium tremens

A dangerous state of alcohol withdrawal that causes violent tremors, hallucinations, rambling speech and hyperactivity. It usually takes place three to four days after very heavy drinking has stopped

Diabetic

Person suffering from a metabolic disorder that reduces the body's ability to control the amount of glucose in the blood

Discrimination

How a person can treat another person or group unfairly, based on their prejudice

Economic factors

Factors such as income and unemployment

GP fundholders

GP fundholders were given a budget each year by the Health Authority to buy services for their patients. The Health Act 1999 abolished GP fundholders

Health and well-being

Health comes from an Old English word meaning *whole*. Health encompasses physical, emotional, intellectual and social well-being. Health and well-being should mean that a person feels positively well and is not just free of disease or illness

Health promotion

Advising others on health and well-being. Health promotion materials help get the message across to people

Human development

Includes physical, intellectual, emotional and social development throughout the various life stages

Informal relationships

Informal relationships are those we participate in because we enjoy them. For example, we may use our leisure time to play football or badminton

Life events

Examples of life events include redundancy, serious illness, disability, divorce or the death of someone close to you

Life stages

The main life stages are infancy, childhood, adolescence, adulthood, early old age and 'older' old age

NHS Trusts
Self-governing health care organisations, such as hospitals, with responsibility for their own budgets

Non-judgemental attitude
Not judging other people's actions

Non-verbal communication
Communication carried out without speaking – we call this non-verbal communication or body language

Nutrient
Anything that feeds or nourishes the body

Nutrition
We describe the content of food in terms of the nutrients it contains – for example, protein, fat, carbohydrate, vitamins or minerals

Passive smoking
People who live or work in smoky atmospheres without smoking themselves are termed passive smokers

Personal hygiene
Poor personal hygiene causes the spread of more diseases than anything else. Use of soap and hot water in washing removes many bacteria from skin. It also removes dead skin cells and oils that provide a food source for bacteria and fungi

Practice nurse
Usually employed directly by a GP practice, where most of their work is carried out. Practice nurses carry out such routine tasks as applying dressings to wounds, taking urine tests and giving injections

Prejudice
Prejudice is when a person prejudges (makes up their mind in advance about) another person or a group of people

Primary Care Groups
Groups set up under the 1999 Health Act to improve the health of, and address health inequalities in, the local community and to develop primary care and community health services in their area

Primary Health Groups
Made up of GPs, community nurses and local authority representatives, Primary Health Groups work with NHS Trusts to plan the health services to deliver prompt, accessible, seamless care to a high standard

Pulse rate
A measure of the heart rate. The average pulse rate is about 70 beats per minute but it may vary according to client group

Purchaser and provider

A *purchaser* is an organisation that buys a service from another organisation; a *provider* is the organisation that provides the service

Referral

There are three ways that a person can be referred to the health or social care services: self-referral, referral through professionals and compulsory referral

Roles

Expected patterns of behaviour that we learn through the socialisation process. We absorb by watching, listening and imitating how we should be, what we should say and how we should act

Safe sex

The main rules of safe sex are: restrict the number of sexual partners; use condoms; and practise good personal hygiene

Self concept

The way a person sees themselves, including not only physical appearance but also the understanding of what kind of person they are

Self-esteem

How people value and see themselves

Social class

A form of social stratification system for putting people into strata or layers such as working class, middle class or upper class

Socialisation

The process whereby we become members of society by learning its various ways and rules. Socialisation starts when we are born and only ends when we die

Socio-economic

Economic factors, such as the amount of income we have and how we spend it, affect how we live, and are linked to social class

Stress

A response to the imbalance between an individual and the demands made on that individual

Substance abuse

The improper use or abuse of any substance – for example, alcohol, tobacco or drugs

Verbal communication

Communicating by talking to other people

Vitamins

Nutrients found in food that are needed in small amounts. For example, vitamins A and D are fat-soluble and are generally found in fatty foods; vitamins B and C are water-soluble and cannot be stored by the body, and therefore daily supplies are needed

Index

Page references in *italics* indicate tables or diagrams